THE

REJECTED STONE;

OR,

INSURRECTION *vs.* RESURRECTION

IN

AMERICA.

BY A NATIVE OF VIRGINIA.

(Moncure Daniel Conway)

Third Edition.

BOSTON:
WALKER, WISE, AND COMPANY,
245, WASHINGTON STREET.
1862.

BOSTON.
PRINTED BY JOHN WILSON AND SON,
22, SCHOOL STREET.

CONTENTS.

PREFACE TO THE SECOND EDITION.

THE discussion of the questions of which this little book treats, always important, is now eminently so, because the Head of the Nation has solemnly invoked the attention of Congress and the People to the subject of Slavery as connected with our present conflict. The victories of our arms, still more this noblest victory, — the word "Emancipation" uttered from the White House, — make the conditions under which the second edition of this work is issued much brighter than those which attended its original publication: but *the* victory is not yet won; justice is not yet accepted for the Head of the Corner. So, with gratitude for the reception the volume has met with, I can only welcome the demand for another edition; and, with a prayer that it may find out those who need it, speed it on its way.

MONCURE D. CONWAY.

CINCINNATI, OHIO, March, 1862.

LORD BACON recommends that all important affairs should be committed first to Argus with a hundred eyes, and afterward to Briareus with a hundred arms. "Things," he remarks, "will have their first or second agitation. If they be not tossed upon the arguments of counsel, they will be tossed upon the waves of fortune."

The hundred arms have laid hold on the American question: whether the hundred eyes have done, or are doing, their work, is doubtful.

The daily press brings to each household its presentation of "the situation," in a military aspect; but the ever-developing moral and historical situation is much neglected, or, for reasons of state, suppressed.

"Make bright the arrows," said the Hebrew prophet. In this age, still more in this controversy, every weapon must think, every missile be winged with intelligence, every shell be fused with fire from God's altar.

It is with a profound conviction that the event of this war is to depend more upon the impregnability of principles than that of fortresses, and that it must be fought from a higher plane than any yet occupied by our forces ere it can be won, that I offer the following suggestions and discussion to the American people.

THE REJECTED STONE.

I.

UNION.

In the popular mind, the brave sufferings of our past, the fruitions of our present, and the visions of our future, as a people, are baptized and consecrated in the name of Union. The very word has thus become a talisman, which, because so long supposed to contain all the secret of our national health and wealth, has gained the command of all the living forces of the New World. The good and strong men who have arraigned the Union have done so critically, not virtually; and now, when the question is no longer on the exegesis of Mr. Hamilton's or Mr. Randolph's remarks in the Convention of '87, but on the right of eminent domain in this country, or any portion of this country, as between Barbarism and Civilization, there is but one party possible among loyal men, — that which would preserve the Union.

But it must be candidly acknowledged in the outset, that, in the sense of the politicians, there is no Union to be preserved. 'Tis only a sad satire to call States "United," wherein that which is felt on one side to be the blot on the national escutcheon is maintained on the other as the governor of the national machinery. It is questionable whether the people mean, by their effort to "save the Union," the same that is meant by some of their proxies. Do they mean thereby the preservation of the right at the South to imprison Northern seamen and landsmen accused of no crime? Do our half-million bayonets gleam to-day to defend and preserve the right to nail up Northern freemen in tar-barrels, and roll them into the Mississippi River? Is it, in short, the Union as it was that the people have with one voice declared must and shall be preserved?

It is only a short time since compromises were proposed and seriously considered by the American people. They were deliberately rejected, even when the manifest alternative was civil war. Why rejected? Our people have not been given to scruples against compromise: they had many interests which civil war would ruin. These compromises were rejected, and the most unimportant guaranties refused, simply because of the utter worthlessness of what they were to purchase; i.e., the Union as then existing. The only promise offered in response to Northern concession was, that things just as they were should remain undisturbed and immutable. But the people of this country had maturely decided that the present edition of the country was not worth stereotyping. Indeed, if it were generally understood that the power of our Constitution naturally results or culminates in any one condition of things which the country has yet known, it is doubtful, if, in the Free States, there would be found ten men unrighteous enough to save it. In fact as far as the *old* Union is concerned, the only arms now defending it are in the South: and they have reason; for it was possessed by the demon of the South, its proper soul drugged into torpor, supposed by many dead.

II.

UNMASK.

THE native glow of the human heart is always for justice. Men have not pæans and hymns and celebration-days for epochs when Wrong triumphed over Right. So Tyranny has found it necessary to incloud the glow of heaven in man, which would else melt every chain.

There is a legend of a youth, who, at a masquerade, became interested to know a certain mask This one he pursued everywhere, the figure being equally intent on eluding him. From room to room, from corridor to corridor, he followed. It mounted the stairway; his feet were swift after it. At length, in a deserted chamber, far away from the music and the dancing, he overtook, and unmasked it with a kiss; but what it was that turned and glared upon him he could never bring his pallid lips to utter, — only that it was a thing not of flesh and blood! So have we followed the figure costumed with the stars and stripes, wearing the mask of Union. Far away from the music and the dance, into the deserted chambers, we followed with heedless infatuation. It is our very kiss that has unmasked it. O God! what monster has been moving in our midst, and touching our hands, under this alluring costume!

Now we see that this Union, whatever those who made it meant it should be, has become the hollow mask of SLAVERY.

The present Secretary of State, just before entering his office as such, said to some friends calling upon him, "Let every man now devote himself to saving the Union." — "With liberty in it," suggested one in the company. "Liberty is always in the Union," replied the future Premier. But so soon as he himself comes into the Union with a little finger of authority, held only in the name of Liberty, *that* Union vanishes like a pricked bubble.

At that recent period, no Union but upon a slavery basis, pure and simple, was regarded as possible. Mark the facts.

Our Republican President himself, elected by a people fondly dreaming that Liberty might be allowed at least an occasional angel's visit to the White House, pleaded earnestly with the South to remain in the Union, on the ground, that, if the Union should go, Slavery must go with it.

The leading men of this administration joined in the warning and appeal, arguing with clearness and force that the Union was the only remaining fetter on four millions of human beings.

"What," said the Secretary of State, — "what but the obligations of the Constitution can prevent the antislavery sentiment of this country from assuming at once the European type, — direct emancipation?"

Coincident were the appeals of clerical Unionists in the North to the Southern wings of their churches. The rivets of your slave's manacle are one with the rivets of the Union! "Separated from the North," wrote Dr. Hodge in the Princeton Review, "a Southern Confederacy of the Cotton-growing States would be at the mercy of the antislavery feeling of the world." Dr. Eliot, born and reared in Massachusetts, minister of the Unitarian Church in St. Louis, implores, in the name of Slavery, that Missouri shall resist Disunion: "Separate Missouri from the Union," he said, "surround her with hostile Free States, and in five years the number of those held to involuntary service would be exceedingly small."

Did the American people know, as they watched with pride their colors floating from the mast where they had nailed them, that those colors were the only ones on earth which could still protect the slave-ship? Yet it is even so. England and France stand able and willing to prevent the slave-trade: but the slave-interest of our country has gained a stern prohibition of the right of searching our vessels; and now any pirate has only to run up the stars and stripes over the smooth deck to protect the horrors of the middle passage underneath. On the 26th of February last, Lord John Russell said in the British Parliament, "This flag" (the American) "has covered a vast importation of slaves. If the Spanish flag had been shown, our cruisers would at once have seized the vessels; but, as they bore American colors, it was impossible to do so."

Of every other flag that floats under heaven, you may be sure that it does not cover the traffic in human beings. Of thine, O Union! we cannot even yet say whether it is protecting a nation's honor or a world's shame.

Think of it, my masters!

Think of America fitted out in the order of God as the Life-ship of Nations; of America with a broad continent for her deck, mountain-ribbed to match any billows, launched forth to respond to the signals that come up from voyagers that can struggle no longer; of America, her true captain chained below, turned aside by mutineers from the perishing to whom she was sent, flaring in the eyes of the world the black flag of the slaver!

Reader, you know how it is at sea when the first big ground-swells come: the passengers mutually disclose what they have been dining on. The Union is always called the Ship of State; and the figure was never so appropriate as now, when she has got out here amid the swelling waves of the popular heart, the fresh gales of Freedom filling her sails and snapping her flag, and all the churches and the parties seized with deadly sea-sickness. There is no doubt now what they've all been fattening on. The vomit is black. We find that the churches have been retaliating upon the native African's fondness for "cold missionary," with an equal devotion to pickled Ethiopian; and that the loaves and fishes at Washington have invariably been eaten with African sauce.

Thus, then, we have overtaken the Mask.

Of a truth, we have discovered it a thing not of flesh and blood.

It is over *that* Union, with its mask fallen, that a raven hovers to-day, with its one word, — "NEVERMORE!"

III.

PILATE.

VAINLY has this nation re-enacted the part of Pilate in his court. The king sat with the robe of power about him, and gave up Jesus to the mob. Then he calls for a basin of water, and, washing his hands

2

therein, declares, "I am innocent of the blood of this just person: see ye to it."

Does that absolve the man whose business on that throne is to protect the innocent? The verdict of the world is sure in the end. For fifty generations, Christendom has gone on repeating, "*He suffered under Pontius Pilate.*"

So this nation, sitting on the throne, and surrendering Humanity to the tyrant and the pirate, has again and again washed its hands and proclaimed its innocence. Relentless posterity will all the same affirm that Humanity suffered under the Pilates — Democratic and Republican — who have ruled in the nation and in the States of the nation, and will not spend a thought on the political basins in which their hands are washed.

The damned spot is in every palm: there is not water enough in all the rivers and lakes of America to wash it out. The time will come when we shall be eager to pour into the basin our hearts' blood, and seek in that to cleanse our hands of the stain fallen on us from the sacred hands we have nailed and the side we have pierced.

Henceforth, brother, if we must be devils, at least we can be honest devils; and if any craven priest or tricky politician tells us that we have nothing to do with the crimes of the Union against man, more than with the widow-burning of Hindoos or the cannibalism of Fijians, shall we not at least tell him — in a devout and Christian-like way — that he lies?

IV.

BETWEEN US BE TRUTH.

WITHOUT doubt, the rule of Slavery in the United States, which began its wane as the century passed its noon, was one legitimate and structural phase of the country. It was the result of certain compromises made by its builders; and freemen had either to endure it as best they could, or, as some of the bravest did, take sides with the stone which the builders rejected, against the whole fabric. But can any man in his senses imagine that men fresh from a revolution for Freedom would have stooped to that narrow gate and straitened way, unless they had seen, or thought they saw, the spacious halls of Liberty in the distance? Would they then and there have for ever sealed the doom of their new-born nation's independence? Nailing up a Republican in a barrel, and rolling him into the river, would then be only a symbol of what our fathers did for the whole nation of Republicans. Had the Union been the mere petrifaction of its most rudimental and unripe condition, a contract for the everlasting retention of its tottering infancy, a compact generating no power of self-conservation amid the emergencies of the future, then the nation would have kicked it off as a Chinese shoe, or limped with premature decrepitude to pay, ere its minority had passed, the debt of Nature, — dissolution. Everywhere the limit of growth is the inauguration of death. But the conservative principle in the Constitution was the resource of POWER which it contained. The people accepted the grub actual with the golden wings implied; and now, when the period of change has come, — now, when the chrysalid throbs with the power which forbids it longer to creep, — Slavery steps forward, and cries, "In the Devil's name, creep for ever, or be crushed for ever!"

True, we agreed to the worm. It was not quite noble; but we did it, and grievously have we answered it. But this, through all, was our apology to the humanity we consented to wrong, — this the one solace to our own hearts in their pain and shame: "The worm is no common worm, but one with an inherent power and right to climb to wings. For the beautiful day of its soaring and freedom, we will bear with its present meanness and devastation."

There is need, that, between the star-spangled banner and the stars with bars, a standard higher than either should be lifted, and on it the ancient motto of the Love that is too great to conciliate, — "BETWEEN US BE TRUTH."

When the people of the South consented to the present Constitution, they gained some immediate benefits for Slavery, as we have seen; but no less did they consent to the possible abrogation of every refuge and cover under which Slavery was permitted to hide.

Accepting that instrument, they consented not only to the election of Abraham Lincoln, but to that of Wendell Phillips, if three-fourths of the American people should so much desire such a result as to change the Constitution, so that Mr. Phillips could swear to support it. South Carolina, in adopting that Constitution, pledged her allegiance to a power which could abolish Slavery throughout the land. For doing all these things, the Constitution contains definite formulas and methods, in its power, by a sufficient majority, to supplant its own provisions. Who does not know, unless it be a Secessionist, that this power in any constitution, of alteration and adaptation, is the measure of its lease of life? England has floated down like an ark over the social deluges of centuries, because her constitution was unwritten, and able to grow with the growing world. "England," said Brougham, "has survived, because she knew when to bend."

In its susceptibility of amendment, the Constitution recognizes the Higher Law, — the only law that never fails to be executed.

An ancient code provided the penalty of death for any one who should propose any alteration of its provisions: the proposer should die, even though his alteration should be adopted. And yet proposers came, and their dying breath winnowed that code in every particular. Our Constitution contains no such bloody barrier to its improvement, though the Apollyon of Lynch-law has sought to extemporize one even in the

Senate-chamber. Whilst wisely securing thoroughness in every radical change, by demanding a majority large enough to place such change beyond suspicion of accicent or caprice, our fathers left a doorway for the higher laws which higher civilization must from age to age enact. Had there been no such doorway, the walls would have been long ago battered in under the steady siege of Civilization.

Observe, then, men and brethren, that, in forming this government, Slavery clutched at the strength of the hour; Freedom relied on the inviolable justice of the ages. They have both had, they must have, their reward. That it was and is thus, is apparent from the very clauses under which Slavery claims eminent domain in this country: they are all written as for an institution passing away. The sources of it are sealed up, so far as they could be; and all the provisions for it — the crutches by which it should limp as decently as possible to its grave — were so worded, that, when Slavery should be buried, no dead letter would stand in the Constitution as its epitaph. It is even so. No historian, a thousand years hence, could show from that instrument that a single slave was ever held under it.

V.

THE ORGANIC LAW.

WHEN the Secretary of State said, "*Liberty is always in the Union*," it was a truth in the guise of indirection. But let us not be misled into supposing the Constitution to be the fortress of Freedom, apart from those who occupy it. Except for the equal right of occupation by the portal of the ballot which it gives to the friends of Freedom, its every gun can be wheeled around against Liberty with much more ease than against Slavery. If the present agitation should do no more than bring about a free and frank discussion of our organic law, and suggest the exigent demand for its improvement, it will be worth more than it has yet cost us, or is likely to. There has existed heretofore a popular delusion, that the absolute and divine right of kings has in America been simply transferred to a paper king; that the Constitution is an inspired document, dealing with every interest of its own or our or any time with exhaustive generalization. "Who can tell," said Cicero, "but that the people may come to believe that these stones and pictures are the gods themselves?" Just that came to pass. So the provisions of our Constitution, which our fathers themselves acknowledged as necessarily partial, and in many regards temporizing, are confused by the majority of our people with absolute laws, and worshipped accordingly.

But, outside of mythologies, Minervas in full armor do not spring from the skulls even of Joves (and, in the remote antiquity of our origin, — some sixty or seventy years back, — all American statesmen become Joves).

History and society repeat nothing more constantly than the maxim of natural science, *Nihil per saltum.*

The Declaration of Independence has been called a series of "glittering generalities." Low as was the spirit in which this phrase was uttered, it is certainly true in a most important sense. That Declaration was a study of the millennium; and that does not bloom on the sapling of one revolution, nor of a thousand. Human brotherhood is in it: the instruments are scarcely invented — surely not tuned — to render that symphony. The men who announced those auroral theories of human rights went home to buy and sell their human chattels as before. The French proverb says, "When the saint's day is over, farewell the saint." The signers of that Declaration did but make us a saint's day; and it is to our credit that we rejoice in it more than in all the days whose transactions became the rafters of the house we live in.

It was a "pattern shown in the mount," after which all things in the plain below were to be fashioned; but no sooner have the tables of the law been given, and the lightnings of revolution amid which they were announced sheathed, than the prosaic exigencies of the hour asserted their qualifying clauses. God is great:

Moses can approach him; a golden calf is more comprehensible to the multitude.

So the fiery Declaration cooled down to the wise and wary Constitution.

It is a maxim of natural science, that things move violently out of their places, calmly in them. Ominous warnings are found in Washington's "Farewell Address;" and our earliest state-papers show that fears of a divorce were expressed at the marriage-altar; which indicate that the equilibrium of elements was even then felt to be imperfect. Under the increasing agitations, the popular mind has been so Union-besotted, that it has gone blindly, deeper and deeper, into the danger it meant to avoid by clinging to the Union. As an ideal, we should have been guided by it to a solid shore: as an idol, we have drifted with it on the breakers.

We may well ponder agitations which report things out of their places. For example, Democracy is the people governing themselves, — that is, making their own institutions; but the provision for the rendition of fugitives binds upon the citizens of Free States, to a certain extent, an institution they have abrogated. It is like forcing a horse to live upon fish. Then, again, Democracy must have equal rights as an atmospheric condition; but, by the constitutional basis of representation, the vote of a large slaveholder may balance that of two or three blocks of a Northern city.

These elements, and one or two more that might be named, are out of their places in a republic; and much of the agitation of recent years may be attributed to the effort of the newly awakened forces of the New World to classify themselves more naturally. But let us not be misunderstood here. *The political situation of the parties to the present war does not depend in the slightest degree upon any defects in the Constitution.* The North goes to the battle-field with a record of constitutional obedience clearer than some of her best friends could wish it. She has bowed her back to the heaviest burdens that could be constitutionally imposed upon her. She has been put to shame in her own gates, through long, weary years; and consented to toil on toward her day of deliverance by the slow, prescribed paths. Fulfilling the hard legal conditions, Freedom had climbed the hill Difficulty raised in her path by the Constitution itself, and was near to the gates of the beautiful palace Success, when Apollyon, mad with envy and hate, broke through his own limits, and prepared his darts at the very door of the chamber named Peace. The constitutional disparagements of Liberty have indeed roused Liberty to higher exertions. She has been more in earnest than if a freeman's vote had been equal to a slaveholder's. The shame of repelling the fugitive from her door has nerved her to the atonement she is now ready to make by the shedding of blood; but there has been no evasion, no overleaping of conditions, no cutting of knots she had agreed to untie. Boston saw the skeleton of George III. exhumed, bone refitted to bone, and the grinning skull crowned in her Court House,—this so often as she surrendered her fellow-citizens to slavery; Cincinnati saw the Tour de Nesle rebuilt; Ohio, under a Republican governor, held the clothes of those who stoned Margaret Garner and her children to death, and said, "Her blood be upon us and our children."

No! Slavery now appeals to arms, because Freedom, in her slow but steady progress, has left no informality, no flaw, which can be seized on to reverse the decision she has gained in any higher court.

VI.

THE REJECTED STONE.

It is the inestimable gain of our present condition, that we have come to perceive a weak point in our organic law,—a stone left out, and that a fundamental one.

A disease in any body always flies to the weakest point of that body, and thus proves what is its weakest point.

Chase the fox, and it will show you the hole in your wall.

On either theory of the Constitution, that which binds it back for ever to the shell it is ready to cast, or that which empowers it to struggle up with the struggling world, — conserving its principle of life in its principle of growth, — our nation's present emergency brings the whole country to the stone which the builders rejected; announcing the irreversible decree, that either we must be wrecked upon that stone, or else that it must be taken as the head of the corner.

That stone is, essentially, JUSTICE.

The form in which it stands for us is THE AFRICAN SLAVE.

The ethnologic African is nothing to us here, nor his place in the scale, nor yet his capacity. Our fact lies in this, that he is inevitably the third party in any contract that can be made between the North and the South. He must be presently recognized as a party to the contract, who has already demonstrated his power to tear it in pieces. We have already had our experience; and, if we do not profit by it, 'tis our own loss. Men who leap from precipices do not imperil the law of gravitation. Obey the truth, and it comes a life-giving sunbeam out of heaven; disobey, and it comes all the same, but now a deadly sun-stroke.

When our national firm was consolidated, the African's name was left off the sign, as his right was left out of the compact; but every year has shown his increasing power in that firm. It is plain, he can be no longer considered even a silent partner. The thunder of his voice mutters under every home in the South to-day. They who hear it turn pale, and say, "Your nation is nothing, and worse than nothing, to us, unless it resolve itself into a police-force for the protection of Slavery. So soon as the monster is denied its daily virgin, it turns to crush us."

Fearful is their sincerity! What they say is credible, as the last words of the dying. Unless the organic law is so amended as to nationalize the code of Slavery, to adopt and foster the institution, the South feels herself to be, and is, in the midst of advancing society, like the prisoner of the Inquisition amidst the ever-encroaching walls of his dungeon, who could compute the minute when they must crush him between them.

And to the North the warning of the African is equally imperative. The North has walked behind to strengthen those who shot their arrows at him, but has found that every arrow was from a Tartar bow: it has returned from its flight to plunge into those who thought to find security in the rear. The North has, in these last years, become a funeral procession following the hearses on which lie a fallen Literature, a tainted Ermine, a putrid Church. On the scholars and the orators, Slavery has brought the plague of the black-tongue.

The Devil's year draws to a close. Bring out the ledgers! See, for every man bought and sold in the South, one was bought and sold in the North!

It is simply useless to accuse the builders on account of their rejection of this stone: it was too large for them to lift. Have we not been dismayed by it? have we not from year to year shrunk from it also? The exigencies of a new and infant nation, requiring before any thing else the necessities of national life and defence, forbade the adjustment of any such question. The true reason why this work was adjourned to us is its commanding extent and grandeur. For those who see in this problem a question of the Negro race, its power or weakness, can do little more than bear a hod for the edifice that is to rise upon this Head of the Corner.

Ages of wrong have, like cold, hard glaciers, graven on this lowly stone the sacred signs of the laws that cannot be broken. Now it stands in our midst the touchstone of every virtue.

There is a print as of nails in the African's hands, and a hollow wound in his side; and, though as a sheep before his shearers he is dumb, a voice comes from behind him, saying, "What for this least one of my brothers you do or do not, you do or do not for me."

The Slavery question is to take many years yet; for it involves the most transcendent laws that infold the earth, — eternal laws of justice and humanity, which have not yet risen, but have only lit up the morning-stars which sing of a new creation. That sneer so lately heard on the street, about "the eternal nigger," is not without its significance: to America he has been, and must continue to be, *eternal,* — even if his race should perish from the planet. Our relations to the

Negro make him for us the sign of eternal justice and inviolable honor. The gift derives its sacredness from the altar. The more lowly and incompetent that race, the more sacred its cause to all loyal men. His plea the Negro can only utter by the tongue or pen of other races; but his silence is more eloquent than any tongue or pen. He is absent from our pews; he is unfit for our parlors: but his absence bears a more withering rebuke to the wrong that has held him down in the ascending world, than his presence. He can only sign his plea with his cross-mark; but it is the indictment of humanity itself against us; and that sign of the cross affixed is the double seal of his ignorance, and of the inhumanity which has caused it. Thus the black man withdraws before the universality of his issue, which becomes that between absolute right and wrong. The verdict he claims is the verdict of man as against the oppression of a class.

Even if we cannot all see that his issue is that of the whole world, we have surely found that it is that of every race comprised in America. In our grief, we remember the warning of St. Pierre, that "man never puts a chain about his brother's neck, but God is sure to put the other end of it around his own." In our first Revolution, we saw that the right to take one pound implied the right to take a thousand: we have required another to reveal that the right to enslave four millions implies the right to enslave thirty Again and again we have shoved aside the importunate, widowed Africa, who came with shackled hand uplifted in petition; and, now that she troubleth *us*, we may avenge her. Her cause has become our own.

Therefore we would avenge her; but would we do her justice?

At this moment, we are inviting the thunderbolt of subjugation by separating our own issue in the war from that of the African as far as possible. This day, were our part of this difficulty settled by the rebels grounding their arms, there would be no difficulty, as far as our rulers are concerned, in consolidating the Union over the prostrate form of the Negro.

But the rebels have no thought of grounding their arms; nor will they, until they see flashing in the sunlight a certain sword which yet sleeps in its scabbard. And it may be long yet before that sword is unsheathed. For to do justice to the Negro is to lay the corner-stone of the Republic of Man. It is nothing less. Therefore this crisis is the most solemn hour that Eternity has dialled on Time; and ages past and coming meet here, and stand unveiled and expectant.

VII.

CONSERVATION.

The preservation of the Union, which is the task now assigned the American people, and of which, fortunately, the evasion is harder than the accomplishment, must necessarily, at first, take the form of disintegration. With destruction all life begins. The birth of the germ is the death of the seed. The Union is under compulsion to find its life by losing it. When the sides of a seed-shell have fallen apart, sundered by the springing germ, vainly shall you endeavor to rivet them together again, and remake the old seed: they can be re-united only by becoming loam for the new form to which they have given birth. Every form, in any kingdom of Nature, contains the necessity of its decay as a form, in the germ of its perpetuity as an essence.

This is a key to the startling evolutions which have so befogged the empirics, and before which the donkeys have not yet found presence of mind enough to bray. How is it, that under the banner which is inscribed "Save the Union" are suddenly found the leaders whose lives have been consecrated to the destruction of the Union in the interest of Freedom? Mr. Everett does not yet comprehend his strange proximity to Mr. Phillips; and the "New-York Herald" is confounded at finding itself under the same flag with the "Anti-slavery Standard." It is because until now the phrase "saving the Union" was the scarecrow of cowardice: now 'tis the watchword of heroism. It meant last year the fatal policy of fostering the ulcer that was eating out the life of the real Union: to-day it means to lay the foundation of a nation that shall be permanent, because founded on the rock of justice.

The soul of Nature has given one wave of its wand over this land; and, in the presence of this Prospero, the semi-brute Caliban and the winged Ariel start forth upon one service. All around us are the treacherous Calibans growling over the work they are forced to do, stung and maddened by the Ariels who sweep on with joy to the loyal task whose fulfilment marks the day of their own liberation also.

Do we realize the straits and sorrows to which a large class of our fellow-citizens are reduced? I refer to the large and much-respected class of *Sitters on the Fence.*

These have come to grief. "Sitting on the fence," once the symbol of earthly ease and repose, has now become the most distressing of attitudes.

Constant abrasions on each side have made the Fence so razor-like, that one who sits on it is in imminent danger of being cut in two.

In the South, if any one attempts to sit on it, he is compelled to ride for eternity upon its top-rail: in the

North, owing to the recent employment of a distinguished maker of rails to repair the Fence, and the consequent shaking, any repose thereon is impossible to any politician less skilful than M. Blondin.

VIII.

COMPROMISE.

THE agitation of the South in awaking from the stupor into which the Black Drug threw her, when new markets raised the price of slaves, learning now, for the first time since she signed the Compact, the nature and extent of the power wherewith it has all along been in gestation, is most natural.

The instinct of Slavery is wiser than the consciousness of the Republican party, which is so eager to deny any dissatisfaction with Slavery where it exists; opposing it only where it doesn't exist.

The naturalists tell us that every animal knows by instinct, and at first sight, the animal that naturally preys upon it. The mouse just born, which has never seen any animal, will show every sign of terror at sight of a cat, whilst calm enough before other animals. The instinct of the Southern mouse tells true when it recognizes that Freedom never yet rested, never can rest, quiet with its eye upon a slave.

It is very plain, that if, in ten years, had the normal progress of the country continued, three-fourths of the people had been found determined on taking advantage of their constitutional authority to abolish Slavery, such a result would not have been outside of the ratio in which the antislavery sentiment has increased since Hale and Julian, twelve years ago, received less than two hundred thousand votes on the platform that now rules in the Capitol.

Slavery, with the keen sense of a savage, lays its ear to the ground, and hears in those ballots falling for Abraham Lincoln the fatal tramp of many centuries, the mustering for liberty of the ages that take no step backward. It does not pause even to listen to the protestations of Freedom's picket-guard, that her grand army will never invade the sacred soil of constitutional oppression ; cares not to inquire whether they are honest or otherwise ; knows better ; prepares to defend every inch of its bloody deck, every fetter in its coffle. Thank God for that savage instinct, which, when as yet there was no North, saved us from the deadly evils that spring from the making of promises that Fate must for ever forbid us to keep !

The Republican party was doubtless sincere in its eager denial of any intent to interfere with Slavery in the States, even through legal and constitutional formulas ; for even our President consented, in his inaugural, to offer this filthy coin, slipped by Seward into his hand, to purchase a Union, when the very fact of its having to be purchased, even with a half-dime, would prove it already gone.

The power which controls the country and the world — the power which has put forth ten thousand parties like summer-leaves, and shed them when their autumn came, itself remaining rooted and fixed in the stratum that changes not — has already exculpated the Republican party from any suspicion of ulterior intent, by raising up a nobler one to take its place. At a little town in Ohio, where they had two poles with party-flags flying from them, the people, when they heard the boom of a shot falling in Fort Sumter, went to the common, cut down the two poles, tore away the flags, spliced the poles into one, which they raised with ONE flag on it. This is a symbol of a process, which, somewhat more slowly, but rapidly enough, has been for some months going on with the parties. The electric power of patriotism is bringing from each some contribution to the forces of Liberty. The Republican party needed this solvent as well as others. It was no sooner in power than it began to go the way of all parties. Hear a parable thereof.

There was a young man, as the story runs, whose mistress was extremely ill. Anxious and distressed, he went forth to seek a physician able to cure her. On the way, he was offered, and purchased at a large price, a talisman, which had the magic quality of revealing to its possessor all disembodied spirits. With this he approached the doors of the most distinguished physicians of Paris. All above and about their doors, he saw, by the aid of his talisman, the ghosts of those who had departed this life under their practice. Spirits with pill-boxes, spirits with syringes, with lancets, with wet sheets, all spurted, and cut at, and sought to douse, the unconscious doctors, whenever they appeared at their doors. Presently the young man, after wandering in despair from door to door of the celebrities, paused before that of a physician, over which he saw two — only two — very mild-seeming spirits. The contrast with the doors of other doctors pleased him. "Here," he said, "must be an able physician. Only two have died under his charge; and they may have been too far gone before he was called in." The young man entered, and told his fear and distress: "O sir!" he cried, "my only hope is in you." — "And why," asked the happy doctor, "do you trust in me?" — "Ah," replied the youth, unwilling to mention his talisman, "have I not heard your reputation for success in difficult cases bruited throughout the city?" — "Good heavens!" exclaimed the astounded doctor, — "my reputation! Why, I have not been in Paris but eight days, and never had but two patients in my life!" The young man remembered the two he had seen over the door, and rushed from the room in despair.

No wonder the country hurried away from such spirit-haunted doors as those of Dr. Democrat, Dr. Whig, and Dr. Know-nothing. But, over Dr. Republican's door, there was a ghost before he had been in Washington a week; and he never had but one patient in his life. He inaugurated his practice in that city by proposing to the States to adopt, as a part of the Constitution, the most essentially unrepublican feature that could be inserted in any organic code; namely, a fetter binding the people for ever from any alteration of their Constitution as it concerns Slavery in the States. Jeff. Davis will never give this nation so deadly a stab as would the adoption of that provision by the people. In twenty-five years, the very swords which now defend the Union would be turned toward its heart.

If Compromise — that old serpent ever coiling about the tree of life — has been baffled this time, it is not because the party in power did not yield to his seductions. Enough secret correspondence went on at Washington, which it will, for a long time, be "incompatible with public (i.e. Cabinet) interest" to publish. (Alas! we need it not: the "Campbell and Seward Letters" are already too much!) It now appears that the serpent only desired time to wound our heel. Four months he got, against the protest of the nation, and planted his fang just where he aimed.

A compromise with the South has now been shown as impossible as a compact with a maniac. It is all the more so when the maniac has a method in his madness, and a sufficient reason for it.

Are men fit to lead and rule the forces now roused into action in this country, who talk of "this wanton and unnecessary rebellion"? Stupid!

There never was a more religiously earnest, deliberate, consistent, and necessary rebellion. Is it not as much the nature and mission of the thorns to spring up and choke the good seed sown in their midst, as it is the nature and mission of the honest soil to bring forth thirty, sixty, or a hundred fold? Slavery has never departed from its normal development. Its exasperation is the legitimated result of the exasperation of Freedom. It is always the sun itself that calls up the cloud that would obscure it.

"The South has been told lies about us and our designs." Not at all. The South understands us better than we do ourselves. They see that politicians have not awakened the forces that have made them, and cannot put them to sleep as they will. They have seen a man, with a price set on his head, setting up his "Liberator" in an attic, with a Negro boy to help him, — now dipping his pen to announce the decapitation of Slavery under the guillotine erected by himself. They have seen millions kneel and weep at the uplifted scaffold of a man who struck at the heart of Slavery, and knew better than the cautious Secretary, who said that the hero was "justly hung," that, the restraints removed, they would have seen then what they saw a week ago, — twenty thousand freemen gathered on the spot where John Brown died and singing, —

> "May Heaven's smile look kindly down
> Upon the grave of old John Brown!"

Already they heard the cartmen and boatmen of New York and Boston singing to the ring of steel, —

> "John Brown's knapsack is strapped upon his back;
> His soul's marching on!"

They counted each new face which came to the Senate or the House to stand for a principle, which, a few years since, it was a disgrace, or worse, to whisper; until from the Illinois grave of Lovejoy, and on the anniversary of his martyrdom, the conviction for which he died was called by two millions of men, and lifted as the standard of the nation.

They have watched, step by step, the steady, unimpulsive progress by which the people of America, against all the interests so often controlling, — the mercantile interest, the church interest, the political interest, the prayer of peace, — marched forward from year to year to the music of Liberty. They looked straight into the eye of Destiny, and saw that the time must surely come when the free tongue of the ballot would be touched with a live coal from the altar of the American heart; and, though over a devastated land, would at length thunder to the world the law of Freedom and Humanity.

They knew that Humanity's eyes are in its forehead, not in its occiput; that revolutions go not backward.

The South was right, entirely right, in seeing that the election of Lincoln was the signing of the death-warrant of Slavery in the Union. It is of no use smoothing matters to the patient who feels the hectic spot burning on his cheek. No doubt, this first Republican Administration would have been more tender with Slavery than others: so do we humor and indulge, to the top of their bent, those whose graves are near.

But on the day when the nation decided for the principle, that Slavery had a right to be treated only as local property, and then with no more favor than other property, it touched the seat of life.

Slave property does not rest on the same basis with other property; and, under the same treatment, must inevitably pass away.

Its recovery, when astray, cannot be trusted to the laws and courts by which recovery of other property is easy.

It is not natural property, but the creature of enactment: consequently it cannot live on indifference. A mother cannot leave the child born without arms to make what way it can along with those who have two. Slavery has grown strong by being the darling of the Government: it can now live by nothing less.

Our leaders cannot yet bring themselves to treat slave-owners with no more consideration than cow-owners or house-owners. Would a general offer his army to recover a flock of sheep which had taken to their heels, affrighted by his advancing army? Would a commander turn aside from an invasion to crush out with an iron hand the army-worm, if it were devastating the wheat of a field by which he was passing? Would any "Order No. 3" be issued to repel a thousand fugitive horses which should escape from a rebel regiment, and approach our lines?

Where confiscation must touch the slaves of armed rebels,—more perilous, as they are to us, than thrice their value in other forms of property,—Congress halts, hesitates, mixes, then, holding its nose, swallows. This overweening tenderness is the meat on which this our Cæsar has fed that he hath grown so great. Mr. Breckenridge truly called it a bill for the abolition of Slavery. Now, wherever our flag makes its way, liberty to every slave must go with it. This is theory, however: actual emancipation comes later. "He found thereon nothing but leaves; for the time of figs was not yet."

In the present conflict, Slavery has been more candid than we could have claimed. It has not, with the Northern traitors, based its secession upon personal-liberty bills. In some regions, it has acknowledged the Fugitive-slave Law to be unconstitutional: but everywhere it has not failed to perceive that any State bill must be considered constitutional, unless the appointed court declares it otherwise; and has craved no such decision, even with a court suited to its purposes. It has not based its movement on any abridgment of territorial rights. It has frankly acknowledged, that its very existence is incompatible with the existence of free government and popular suffrage. The ballot-box is its coffin. It demands girdling this year: it may demand hewing down the next. It certainly will.

In what attitude does all this place the North?

A mother fled from Moscow in a sledge drawn by an Arab steed. At her breast, folded warm from the cold of the bitter night, she held her babe. Then came the wolf upon her track, with its terrible howl. Fast and faster sped the sledge over the frozen snow; but the hungry wolf gained on her. Piece by piece, she cast behind all the provision she had: the wolf devoured each, but, with hunger only whetted, rushed onward after the mother and her child. And now, when it was close upon her, she unwrapped the babe that nestled so near her heart, and cast it to the wolf.

Unnatural mother! would it not have been better, than thus to have purchased for thyself a life of shame, to have turned thyself to grapple with the wolf, and committed thy babe to the Arab steed and to God?

'Tis but a picture of America, with hungry Slavery howling after her. Swift and relentless, it has pursued her. To it she has cast territory after territory; to it she has cast her treasures, and much of her best blood. She has seized from weaker nations around her that with which she thought to satiate the monster: she has seized the panting fugitive, there with halo of divinity about him, and torn him from the horns of God's altar, to cast to the wolf. Insatiable, it presses nearer, and prepares for the final leap.

And now the question is, Shall America cast to the wolf her own sacred child, — Liberty?

No!

O my brothers! a thousand times, No! Let the mother, let America, turn to cope with Slavery, though she be torn asunder; but let the holy child Liberty, over all, be saved!

This, then, being the moral situation of the two parties, each knowing the very existence of the other to be its own destruction, the very field of compromise is the field of battle.

Freedom and Slavery have been hugging each other so hard, that it has grown to a death-hug.

We need not fear negotiation too much: in this stage of the conflict, any compromise will be only a flag of truce. Some timid officials, wishing to get out of the region of "villanous saltpetre," may send out such a flag, and gain an armistice for a few months or years; but the end cannot come until Slavery or Liberty lies slain.

It is written, "Righteousness and Peace have kissed each other." Sixty centuries of experience have added, "Unrighteousness and War are forever linked together."

Can any compromiser promise us, as the result of his plan, any thing else than the old "irrepressible conflict"? You must cut the heart out of every thinker and reformer in America ere you get any thing else; and resistance is the multiplication-table of Reform.

Is this, then, as some affirm, the swelling of a flood that shall presently subside again?

A traveller came to a river; and, being unable to ford

it, he sat down on its banks, saying, "I will wait until the river has flowed by." He waited long; he built him a house there; and when the traveller's bones were traces of white lime, and the house marked only by the luxuriance of weeds on its site, the river was still flowing by.

Let America scorn to adjourn for her children in the future the task now assigned her: she is too old in sorrow already not to know that a postponement is all she can effect, even if the Kind Hand has not removed that temptation. "The cup that my Father hath given me to drink, shall I not drink it?" Not to be evaded, nor dashed aside, nor spilled, was it given.

Hail, hail to thee, Messiah of nations, — thou who comest from Edom with thy garments dyed red! With thee go the blessings, for thee rise the prayers, of noble hearts all over the world, as thou goest forth steadfastly to tread the wine-press prepared by Destiny for thy feet, knowing not the wine that shall come, only that it shall make glad the heart of man. O my Country! there is a path that leads from Gethsemane, Garden of Agony, up to the snow-pure summit of Tabor, Mount of Transfiguration. There shall thy nobler children rear for thee the tabernacles of the Past, the Present, and the Future.

IX.

BROKEN.

In an old law-book — older than the Constitution, or the Missouri Compromise, or the Omnibus Bill — it is written of the Rejected Stone, "*Whosoever shall fall on this stone shall be broken; but, on whomsoever it shall fall, it will grind him to powder.*"

Against the strong arm of this Universe hold out as we may, at length to its behest we must be broken. The Phœnician replies to the lightning with arrows: at last, men return their arrows to the quiver, and lift the lightning-rod for protection. Canute lashes the advancing tide: at last, men note the high-water mark, and build far enough beyond it. So we yield in the end.

Broken! 'Tis no threat; 'tis no violence. The shuck of the wheat is broken under the flail, that the grain may be separated; the grain itself is broken, that bread may be kneaded. Even so it is with nations: under the flails of God, they, too, must lie; upon his mill-stone, for ever revolving, they must be broken.

> "Though the mills of God grind slowly,
> Yet they grind exceeding small."

In the pride of our progress, in the ruddy strength of our youth, we lost the one thread that links the present to the past: we neglected the ever-accumulating tradition, that Justice alone can really exalt a nation; that

Justice, being overturned, will overturn. A few years ago, our leading statesman announced that there was a higher law than any human code. An angry echo from every point of our national compass growled back upon him; the majority of the nation defied the supreme right, until he who brought the tables of that higher law was compelled to break them. Our fathers, kneeling with reverence before the sublime fact, still fresh in the wonder of nations, that a handful of men had been able to repel the strongest of nations, simply by the power of rectitude in their cause to engender superhuman strength, had recognized the law higher than that which they framed, and left open the door of amendment whereby new revelations might enter. But our nation declared for nullification of the laws of God. It declared for injustice. It announced that the black man had no right that the white man was bound to respect. It enacted that every American, when called on by an arch slave-hound, should at once get down on all-fours, and become a slave-hound. It went on from whorl to whorl of corruption; it drew near to the bottomless pit; when suddenly the Great Hand rescued it from the nearly completed death, and cast it upon a glorious Revolution to be broken.

Did we think to gain any thing by consenting to sell our brother to the Egyptian, heeding not his cries and tears? Lo! a mighty famine is in the land, and the lost Joseph is seen clothed with the power of locking up all the produce and wealth of the country.

Begin on the lowest plane, — for some are oxen, and must be led by hay, — and ponder well the "broken" fortunes of this country, resulting from its proud conceit that it could outwit the equity of the Universe. A pre-Æsopian fable relates that there was a fox who espied a garden of luscious grapes. To this garden, however, he could find but one opening; and that was too small to admit his somewhat portly dimensions. The grapes were very tempting: what could Reynard do? He hit upon a plan: he would fast until he became lean enough to get through the hole to the garden. Each day he tried, and on the third day found himself sufficiently reduced to enter. Judge how the hungry, half-starved rogue enjoyed those delicious grapes. But, hark! there is the sound of a farmer's voice: surely that was the distant bay of a dog! Master Fox finds that his plan is not altogether safe: the close fence was built to *exclude* foxes. He hastens to the hole; but, alas! he finds that the hole which was large enough to admit a fox that had been fasting three days is too small for a fox full to the mouth of grapes. What can he do? Another ominous bay of the distant hound decides him: he must needs fast three days more; and then, just as the gardener and his dog entered, *he managed to escape, just as lean a fox as he was when he reached the delicious grapes.*

Thus it was that the Northern fox entered the Southern cotton-field. On what a low diet he must put himself! "We have some prejudices against the buying and selling of men, which don't go easily into a plantation." Mr. Webster replies, "You must conquer your prejudices." Good heavens! who would have thought that men could starve out to such an extent the love of justice, the conscience, the manhood which they had inherited! Yet the State would not make the hole bigger, and the Church did not tempt them with any other viands to abstain; and at length the North was morally reduced enough to get on its knees, and creep into the small aperture to King Cotton's dominions. Speedily the Yankee fattened on the grapes; great flakes of Wall Street stuck out on his sides; State-street layers puffed out his eyes, so that he could scarcely see!

But the day of danger looms up. When Master Fox gave up soul and heart to get amongst these Southern grapes, he did not mean to give up *himself;* but here Slavery is dogging him also. We need not pursue further the history of the humiliating necessity which we are now undergoing: the North is now disgorging all that it gained by years of shameful compliance with the evil of the South and the crime of the nation; and it must continue to pay down dollar on dollar until it reaches some new Plymouth Rock, as lean as if it had never seen the garden of the South, but rich, let us trust, in the experience that will never again let the seeds of the "Mayflower" wither as they spring up, because they have no depth of earth.

The Devil seemed to be the shrewdest of Yankees:

now the old proverb is remembered, *The Devil's an ass.*

"Thou hast conquered, O Galilean!" said dying Julian the Apostate. The North may, *and will,* now collect the bones of her great-browed children who yielded because she said "Yield;" the fallen pillars of her crumbled church; her children whose wounds yet smoke fresh from the stab of Slavery; — and, broken now upon the stone she so long refused, shall write as their epitaph, —

Vicisti, Humanitas!

X.

THE PRIVATEER.

A CRY comes up to the ear of America, — a long, piercing cry of amazement and indignation, — recognizable as one which can come only when the profoundest emotions of the human pocket are stirred. The privateers are at large! They have taken away my coffee, and I know not where they have laid it. They have taken my India goods with swords and staves. For my first-class ship they have cast lots.

Was such depravity ever known before? So long as it was a human soul, launched by God on the eternal sea, that they despoiled; so long as it was only a few million bales of humanity captured; so long as it was but the scuttling of the hearts of mothers and fathers and husbands and wives, — we remained patient and resigned; did we not? But coffee and sugar! — good God! what is that blockade about? To seize a poor innocent sloop! — has Slavery no bowels? And its helpless family of molasses-barrels! — can hearts be so void of pity? Slavery must end. The spirit of the age demands it. The blood of a dozen captured freights crieth to Heaven in silveriest accents against it.

Brothers, there is a laughter that opens into the fountain of tears.

Can you tell me, you ship-owners and rich merchants, for how many cycles the coffee-berries ripened and fell ere came that marvel, a human hand, to gather them for you? Will you ponder the stretch of the ages when fields of sugar-cane rotted to bring on new growths, and these to bring on others, to prepare merely the sod worthy to support the foot-sole of the man whom you have seen nailed up, body and mind, in your sugar-hogshead, without complaint, so long as the sugar came safely to hand? Have you not confused things a little, imagining that in nature the dusky man was for loam, and that the culminating glory and flower of the universe is Cotton? How else shall we interpret your years of silence and calmness when only men and women were in the hands of the privateer, and your outcry when old metals and juices and vegetables are imperilled?

Yet, too thankful that even thus the heart of trade is moved, one who, through many weary years, has watched the torches kindled at the Light of lights flickering their lives away in the dark caverns underneath Trade's gay saloons, cannot repress delight at the gay privateer. God speed thee, rakish "Sumter;" and thee, swift-pouncer "Nashville"! May Heaven's blithest breezes fill your sails, until your arrows of conviction have penetrated every unconvinced heart! We have got our Scripture interpretations fearfully confused: you peppery missionaries will shed brilliant exegetical light over the land. We shall have revised views from President Lord on the curse of Canaan; and anti-piratic commentaries on the case of Onesimus, from Nehemiah. Our ethnology has become somewhat foggy: your arguments will be stronger than the now fashionable ones of Nott and Gliddon. We may discover a link in the races lower than the Negro, without travelling with Du Chaillu. God speed thee, brave privateer!

So long as African Slavery runs the blockade of the parties and churches of America, so long may the privateer run the blockade of the Southern coast with safety!

XI.

A FOREIGN POWER.

THE promptness with which the Secretary of State has expressed the position of our Government on our transatlantic relations has elicited the warmest commendations of the people. It has been distinctly announced, that in this contest we will submit to no interference and accept no help from foreign powers.

Especially none from the Powers Above!

Toward the last foreign Powers the cold shoulder has been turned in a way to rejoice the hearts of the "New-York Herald" and the "Boston Courier," and many others, who have long insisted on the strict application of the Monroe doctrine to the government of God, whose aims at encroachment on this continent they have watched with such a jealous eye.

Yet it is less than doubtful if we can conquer without them, or irrespective of an alliance with them.

Except as the two are symbols of other facts, we suppose that humanity at large is entirely indifferent whether the individual residing in the White House for the next four years is named J. Davis or A. Lincoln. If these two represent inferior and superior principles, — so that, as one or the other rules there, the shadow moves forward or backward, marking progression or retrogression on the dial of civilization, — then the world is pledged to the superior. But suppose that to England, for instance, there are presented simply two jarring political — purely political — interests, in the names of the two Presidents; one representing the integrity of the boundary-line of a rival nation, the other the independence of a nation not her rival, and on which she is dependent for cotton. The government, obeying its first instinct, self-preservation, as our own does, stands perfectly justified in taking sides with that party in which her interest is most involved. England has herself set up the standard of emancipation, and to that her people would hold her; but where that principle is not only not involved, but distinctly disclaimed, the people will leave the government to the normal influences of the cotton-mill. They do perfectly right. The antislavery men of Europe have little reason to choose between governments supported by Caleb Cushing, B. F. Butler, and the "New-York Herald," on the one hand, and Yancey, Rhett, and Jeff. Davis, on the other. It is brought before Europe as a purely political question; and we cannot, without a contemptible conceit, expect any element to determine the attitude of Europe toward it higher than POLICY. Is not popular government involved? Assuredly: but Europe has decided already that popular government is not good; equally it has decided that cotton *is* good.

Now let us trace this same principle as it decides our relation to the transmundane Power.

Our Congress requested the President to appoint a day of humiliation, fasting, and prayer; and he did so: which shows that we have rather more disposition to conciliate this than any other foreign power. This was doubtless due to a late defeat. One is reminded of the psalm our fathers sang:—

"Jeshurun he waxed fat,
And down his cheeks they hung:
He kicked against the Lord his God,
And high his heels he flung."

Jeshurun was reduced. We also have been reduced, certainly in a military, and we trust in a moral sense. When any fruits of this repentance are brought forth, we shall be glad to record the indications. Thus far, we stand fighting for as purely a selfish end as the rebels of the South.

No doubt there are thousands of men North, and with our army in the South, who plead and fight for justice and freedom, not only for the electors of Mr. Lincoln, but also for men of every color. These maintain the Government, because they hope, that, in its contest with the slaveholder, the slave will be freed. But should the star-spangled banner ever float on the shores of the Gulf, and still over African slaves, the hearts of thousands would once again freeze toward this nation, and the flag of Disunion float in the North, with thousands around it where hundreds were before.

Our President and his Premier have given us our

watchword: they have told us, that between Slavery and Freedom there is an "irrepressible conflict." If the Union with Slavery in it is regained, all will know that it is but the lull of the volcano.

Thomas Jefferson once said, that, if the South were ever to witness an insurrection of slaves, there was no attribute of God which could take the side of the oppressor in that contest. The leading commanders of this war against an insurrection initiated their entrance into the regions of Slavery by a promise of crushing out with an iron hand the insurrection of slaves: in other words, should these Negroes take side with our men in a struggle of life and death, they would be shot down for helping us! Nearly every general proclaims that no fugitive shall enter his lines. Our President, in the midst of a slaveholders' insurrection, and on the blessed Fourth of July itself, sends a message to Congress, in which Slavery is not remotely alluded to.

Not long ago, a distinguished friend of the Republic of Haiti, in company with a very able and learned Senator, entered the office of a very wise and diplomatic Secretary of one of the departments of this Government: whereupon a scene like this occurred: —

Senator. Mr. Secretary, permit me to introduce you to Mr. A. B., a friend of the Haitian Government, and authorized to represent the same to a certain extent.

Secretary. How do you do, Mr. A. B.?

A. B. Quite well, I thank you.

Senator. The Haitian Government now naturally hopes that the success of Republicanism secures the recognition of her republic.

A. B. She is ready to send her minister at any time.

Secretary (*twisting uneasily in his seat*). Really, gentlemen, this is a very grave and difficult question; and I have not leisure to consider it.

Senator. A *difficult* question? 'Tis but a scratch of your pen.

Secretary (*twisting three times in his seat*). But, sir, — really, sir, — I — I —

A. B. Oh! do not let us press it, if the Government is averse to it.

Secretary. The fact is, gentlemen, Washington cannot receive a black minister.

(*Exeunt Senator and A. B. with "Good-mornings."*)

The Republican Administration had answered Republican Haiti in the very words of Henry A. Wise, when, a nation freed by her own right arm, she vainly appealed to America for recognition, as America had a few years before, and under the same circumstances, appealed to other nations.

The intrenchments about Washington may be very complete; but mark this: *Washington is not safe until a black minister can be received there!*

Now, whilst we are speculating as to the possibility of our blockade being raised by France and England, would it not be well for us to see if we have not weakened our cause and our force by completely disowning the only moral element in this conflict?

We have made, or are in danger of making, four millions of disappointed enemies in the South, whom we might have counted on as our friends in any emergency. Freedom is first with the black, as with every man: next to that, the evil he knows, against that he knows not. Every Negro returned to his master — to be made an example of what treacherous Negroes may expect in these times — has sown amongst his comrades the seeds of hate and revenge against our army.

We have disheartened many of our noblest and best young men, by degrading, with a taint of man-hunting and oppression, the banner and the cause.

We have paralyzed the pulses of the lovers of equality and liberty all over the world, which were ready to beat toward us with a steady tide of sympathy and encouragement. How could Victor Hugo or Garibaldi extend his hands to a general, who, with the very weapon with which he is defending his own liberty, is ready to crush others who would seek theirs?

We have lost the battle of Manasses, and with it the prestige of a first victory and the order of an army, chiefly because General McDowell's colorphobia must cut off the Negro's hope, and with it his own only source of information. It was a crime and a blunder.

In refusing to recognize Haiti, we have shrouded the

one light that might now be shining over the darkest problem of this war.

Would it not be a curious case of poetic justice, if, in a year from now, we should witness a "situation" somewhat like the following?—

1. The United States calling on the slaves of the South, to whose bondage she has so long been a party, whose possible freedom by confiscation she reluctantly approved, to save her entire people from subjugation.

2. The United States begging Haiti to help her sustain and shield millions of manumitted women and children, and invoking a black minister at Washington.

The army of the United States is, without doubt, fighting for the liberty of the slave; but so also is the army of the Confederate States. Both are, by compulsion, hastening the day of freedom (but that is scarcely more our object than it is theirs). Indeed, the Southern army has done more of this indirect service to humanity than our own. With both it has been involuntary. There is a Power behind both thrones at work. Freedom sits above, in calmness and light; and we know her star cannot recede below the horizon: but whether she is to be advanced the next step by a dreadful retribution to the recreant North, or by the conquest of the South, is, alas! yet doubtful. Again and again have strong governments, not built upon the head corner-stone of Justice, been buried under the splendor of their own ruins, that humanity at large might have another monument to say, "REMEMBER!"

Were our cause sanctified by any universal principle, the arm of God, whose sinews are the true hearts of the whole world, would be folded about us. "But," it is replied, "we are fighting for the principle of free suffrage: it is bullets arraigning ballots." Yet scarcely can free suffrage be called a principle. It is an institution yet on trial in the world: it has yet to make its cause good at the tribunal of Reason. Freedom of the ballot is not necessarily good in itself: if it result in perpetuating injustice or in anarchy, it proves itself a wrong principle. New-York City has had to ask the State Legislature to select her municipal officers. England may well point to her superior freedom under limited suffrage. Her members of Parliament are not assassinated; her Queen does not have to pass from Scotland to London in disguise; there is no county of her kingdom where her most radical orator is debarred an entrance on penalty of tar and feathers. All these evils have for years co-existed with our popular suffrage; *and our Republican Administration would hardly have molested one of them, had the South not precipitated this Rebellion.*

Therefore we still maintain, that, as far as our Government is concerned, — that is, saving a reserved purpose among the unofficial masses whose power is yet to be measured, — we have no aim in this conflict that makes our cause the cause of Destiny, or our success any necessary step in the progression of the world.

XII.

MANASSES.

It is said that one of our army chaplains had prepared a discourse on the text, "Manasseh is mine." It was never preached. At daybreak his regiment was marching forward, with the hope of preaching the same text from the cannon's mouth. But the text has remained a vision in the Psalms.

Manasses is a symbol. The assault and the courage of it, the repulse and the shame of it, symbolize with unerring accuracy a certain moral status of our nation, consequently of its army, which, by the conditions of the universe, did not deserve Manasses, and did not obtain it. Why were we defeated there? We had poor generals. Why had we poor generals? Why was Patterson enabled by his cowardice or treachery to make our disaster sure, after McDowell, by blunderingly marching in the dark, had made it probable? Both of these men were known as life-long cringers to the men they were sent to fight. If John Brown had been with a United-States army at Harper's Ferry, would he have been animated with what seems to have been Patterson's one aim, — to return his young volunteers safe to their parents unharmed? Not so did John Brown return his own sons. If Montgomery of Kansas had been at Fairfax, would he have scorned the only medium of intelligence and real help, — the fugitive Negro?

Why were these men, who had proved themselves moral cowards, set to control the forces of Liberty? The Administration took them because the country was not up to furnishing, or standing by, better men. The men who would unweariedly, sleeplessly, with the fire-heart of Peter the Hermit and the iron nerve of Cromwell, have pressed upon and taken Manasses on that Sunday, were men whose appointment would have returned on the Administration a storm of indignation. The country would have been divided, and perhaps surrendered.

Had the country been up to a victory at Manasses, it would have been previously up to having Charles Sumner for President.

But let us search a little further. We have seen that we were outgeneralled because we had half-hearted men to lead our forces. Our soldiers fought bravely, earnestly, and had almost won the day. Why that panic? The intrenchments of the enemy were perfect: our soldiers conquered one battery, only to find themselves at the mercy of two covering it. It had been impossible that Panic could have stormed our army, if Despair had not first weakened it. Our army fought long after every soldier was convinced that they would never occupy Manasses that day.

There were long months, when, it is known, there were few if any batteries or forces at Manasses. Only give me time enough, and I will make any hen-coop impregnable to all the artillery now on this continent. The entire defences of that pass were reared by a most culpable fault on the part of our military and civic leaders, who will stand on the page of History which records that day, as parties to a base deception of the American people. It is now evident that they began this contest on a theory radically different from that which the people had determined was the only one consistent with their national honor. The people were willing to trust them with the method, so long as it was understood that the object to be reached was assigned by them exclusively. Deliberately and absolutely, the people had decided that there should be no new guaranties to Slavery; that there should be no compromise, however infinitesimal; that this issue should fairly and squarely be an acceptance of the gauntlet thrown at their feet by the South. Yet there succeeded the uprising of the people a delay, which, under their very eyes, was improved by the enemy to make Virginia one large masked battery.

There is no question of military tactics and stratagem here,—only a question of common sense and honesty. The men who repulsed drilled regulars at Concord Bridge did not wait for large arrays, fine uniforms, and months of drill. Nay, determination and rapidity had already done for us in Missouri what slowness and Hardee have undone for us at Washington; and would have so continued, had not Washington stretched its red tape into Missouri. These men at the South were even more undisciplined than ours. We should have been, so far, equal. They were our superiors in one thing alone: they had stolen the means of putting a battery on every square acre of their frontier. To fight at once, we were stronger in numbers, and as well drilled: to delay until they were fortified was to make us inferior; the axiom being, that one man behind the trenches equals four outside. The Secessionists of Maryland and Missouri have publicly declared, "We were conquered only by being surprised." Virginia might have been to-day joining in the same confession.

Meanwhile, about all this unfathomable strategy at Washington, — which reminds one of Dr. Cudworth, who, in his contest with the atheists, stated their argument so strongly that he couldn't answer it himself, — there were indications that this delay was more for diplomatic than for military reasons. No traitor was treated as if we were at war. Mr. Breckenridge, in his seat in the Senate, taunted the Government that it had not dared to treat seized rebels as by nations they are treated. The people saw their own soldiers severely and ignominiously punished for offences in the camp, — offences half induced by the demoralization of the delay,

— whilst spies and assassins were released on their already perjured parole.

It became probable to large numbers in this country, who naturally hesitated to express their suspicion, that TWO MEN at Washington — the one in the military, the other in the civic department, each a possible President and hitherto associated with that office — were running a race, each hoping to loom up before a re-united country as A GREAT PACIFICATOR.

Equally were these people convinced that their President was entirely trustworthy, and that no such base pacification could be carried on without his being deceived with the rest of the people.

The suspicion increased when it came out that Mr. Seward had held correspondence with Judge Campbell, and that a quasi armistice had been made at Pickens, of which our President was "imperfectly informed."

The suspicion spread like a contagion that we were deceived. The Government gave no response; no act was done, no traitor hung, to show that the Government meant what the people meant; until at last, the misgiving of our earnest masses becoming intolerable, they uttered their whole heart in that noble war-cry, "FORWARD TO RICHMOND!"

The "Tribune," which was the tongue worthy to utter it, did indeed bow to the storm which always meets the Cassandras who utter too soon what all see presently: but it will one day claim that watchword as the dearest laurel among the many it has nobly earned in this conflict; and the people will one day remember those who told them the truth at risk of their own displeasure, and as long as they could hear it

It was not its fault, nor that of the people for whom it spoke, that stupid or selfish men, and deceivers of the nation, perverted those words into "Forward to Richmond half harnessed! Forward whilst your regiments are in camps all over the North! Forward on empty stomachs! Be sure you take but one man to their three! Be sure you depend for re-enforcement on a man whom the mob of Philadelphia had to force into showing his colors!"

No loyal heart in America should have failed to recognize the plain and ominous tones concentred in that war-cry. It meant, — and many a tricky, trembling diplomat in Washington knew that it meant, — "We, the people of America, are determined for once that we will not be deceived. We do not deplore, but welcome, the storms that are now to sweep away the refuges of lies which politicians have been building out of the rights and honor of the nation. Gentlemen at Washington, civic and military, we have arisen in our might. Each family has with tears of agony, but no less eagerly, laid on the altar its first and fairest fruits. We have, rather than offer a compromise of right and honor, surrendered wealth; nay, some of us, the bread on our tables. We have shown you that we are in earnest. *We have yet to see one fact at our Capitol indicating that you are in earnest as we are.* These men you release

on parole we regard as the murderers of our country. These men you write billets to we regard as the would-be assassins of our husbands, brothers, fathers, and sons. We will not be cheated. *We distrust your moral position toward this Rebellion.* No defeat that can befall us on our way to Richmond can be so bad as being defeated by some patchwork of compromise in our purpose of settling this issue with the South once and for ever. We demand, then, that by some decisive blow, even if it recoil upon us, we shall be utterly committed to this war. We demand that the chasm shall be made so complete, that the most abject trifler, who desires to bridge it with a compromise, shall see that his effort would only sink him in the abyss. Therefore, forward to Richmond!"

All this was in that war-cry, which is to be uttered yet again, and, though with the united voice of the country, with no more nobility than it possessed at first.

When General Scott heard of the defeat at Manasses, he, with great excitement, said that the President should depose him as a coward, because he yielded to this popular pressure. General Scott is not physically a coward. Is he a moral coward? Shall we take him at his word? History records, that a great commander wrote after a defeat, "I have lost a great battle, and entirely by my own fault." In saying this, he gained a greater victory than he lost. Had as sincere and great a spirit commanded at Washington, we believe the country would have received some such message as this:—

"To the People of the United States.

"We, some of your official leaders, have lost you a great battle by our own fault, as far as that fault can be traced to any individuals; which arises from the general corruption of the Government through the malaria of Slavery. When you and your President decided to fight for this Government, we, your public servants, tacitly meant to pacificate and compromise. Acting under this purpose, we gave to you, as a reason for delay, a military pretext. We had no doubt that the South would compromise. They secretly encouraged us to think so; until, when it was too late to remedy our mistake, they showed that their desire for peace was a feint to get time for fortification. When we came to see for the first time definitely that the question must be settled by arms, the nation was already demanding that our delay should end. It was natural that they should so demand. But our first deception could, unless openly confessed, lead only to the defeat of our forces. We could not muster courage to acknowledge the result of our folly, — to say, 'The advance which was feasible two months ago, has, by our delay for negotiation, been rendered impossible. Our honest reply to your "*Forward to Richmond!*" is, that it cannot be done for six months or more, without too much cost; and to advance now would be to wash out a political deception in the blood of brave men.' We had not the moral courage to say it: the fatal result came."

The People reply: —

"Whether the people decide that you gentlemen who hold power under this administration are the right men in the right place, or the opposite, they cannot allow the blame to fall on you for a default which is much more their own. They remember that a wise man affirmed, 'The people are always correctly represented.' Their leaders, military and civic, had every reason to suppose that a people, who have for so many years submitted to having their honor bought and sold by their representatives, had still their price. Though now, 'a nation born in a day,' they abhor their former stupidity and insensibility toward Human Rights, no less than their own self-respect, yet they cannot reasonably complain that these newly unsealed fountains have not, as yet, cleansed the Augean stables of Washington. Therefore we set up our memorial-pillar at Manasses, on it writing, 'Here outraged Humanity was avenged upon a nation, that, from the day of its own liberation, heard the scourges that fell, heard the cries of the stricken, and heeded not, but went on in ignoble rest, until the very sword which guarded its own liberties had rusted in its scabbard.' Therefore we take to ourselves the reproach you have heaped on yourselves, to bear it with you; and, if we call new leaders to your places, it is not for punishment, but it is another effort to make ourselves understood at Washington. It must be there known that we, the people, are in earnest; that we are absolutely determined that this Rebellion shall be crushed, and that in no case shall one-half of this continent be given over to the dominion of Slavery and Barbarism; and that whosoever shall put himself in the way of this purpose shall be swept off as by a flood."

Here let us end this sad chapter,—as painful to him who wrote it as to any who shall read it.

XIII.

BETH-EL.

THIS was the name that the patriarch gave to the place where he came a wanderer. There the sun went down, and he slept with a stone for his pillow. In that night, over that stony pillow, hovered the angels; and in the morning "he took the stone that he had for a pillow, and set it up for a pillar." From his hard lot uprose his strength.

Hard was the pillow given at Manasses, upon which America must rest her head. Is there no heavenward ladder stretching up from that grief? Can she not also take her stony pillow, and set it up for a pillar of future strength? "Experience," says Carlyle, "does charge dreadfully high school-wages; but she teaches as none other." To the same end, Burns's cheery verse: —

> "Though losses and crosses
> Be trials right severe,
> There's wit there, you'll find there,
> You'll get no other-where."

The first and most important lesson inculcated at Manasses is, that *God is* NOT *on the side of the strongest battalions.*

I know that Napoleon said He *was;* but I also know, that, soon after he began to act on that principle, his Battalion-Providence took him to perish on a small rock off the coast of Africa.

There was a time when Napoleon's battalions were arrayed on the side of God: his eye was filled with the coronation-day of Humanity, not of himself. Then, indeed, he was the Man of Destiny; for Freedom marches to the drum-beat of Destiny. Then it was that Beethoven, lover of the people, wrote the "Symphony for a Hero." But soon one brought the old composer tidings of his idol, which caused him to leap from his seat, and tear the symphony, and cast it into the fire: then, with tears, he sat down and wrote the "Funeral March for a Hero," who, as a person, was still living: alas! he lived no more for Man. The Eternal Thought he demanded should shape itself to his battalions. So the halo of Napoleon faded to a diadem.

There is nothing arbitrary or specially providential in all this. He lost his faith in the power of ideas, in the tremendous power of enthusiasm for a high cause; forgot that the sword that seemed to translate the lightning, when striking for eternal Truth and Right, was but a piece of steel, or less, when carving a throne for a man, even though that man were Napoleon. Again and again, the lesson has been assigned us to learn. Xerxes, advancing upon Greece with his countless host, does not find that God is on the side of the strongest. The same testimony was borne at the baptismal blood-font of this nation, and the world called on to observe how three millions had successfully repelled for eight years the strongest nation on earth, and at last brought it to terms, simply because their cause bore with it the inspiration of Liberty.

It seems that we needed Manasses to remind us of it once more.

"What! was the cause of the rebels, and not that of our nation, the cause of Liberty?"

Let us not fear to face the facts; most of all, this chief one: *They were fighting for their liberty.* True, it was *their* liberty; the liberty of Wrong, the free course of Anarchy, the untrammelled rule of Passion, the uncurbed privilege of trampling the most sacred rights and hopes of mankind; a liberty which the laws of this universe for evermore deny. Still, mark: this blow for animal liberty calls up the animal ferocity and strength, which can be mastered only by an equal passion and fortitude for the higher liberty. Fanaticism is only second in strength to inspiration; and we can conquer in this war, only when the love of Humanity inspires us as fully as the love of Slavery inspires the South. Enthusiasm for bunting; interest in a boundary-line; concern for the control of the Mississippi; "institutions bequeathed by our fathers;" "the glorious fabric of our Union,"—I warn you, my countrymen, that, at whatever Manasses these *alone* meet the arms that fight for the kingdom of Oppression, they will be swept away as by a blasting sirocco.

Let us follow the approved maxim that bids us learn from our enemy, and sit at the rebel's feet a moment. See how he fights for Slavery! See how pitiless he is to the enemy of Slavery! Do you live in a Slave State: say one word against the institution, and see if the hearts that knew your childhood do not freeze to ice, and if the arms once twined about you will not be drawn to strike! Over all the appeals of relationship and affection; over all the claims of brain to think, or tongue to speak; over wasted humanity, Saharas of ignorance, over the interests of property,—OVER ALL, the Slave-god sits amidst his devotees. He has his martyrs, as much as Brahm or Jehovah. The parallel drawn between the warfare of Sepoy and Southerner is not fanciful: all races fight so for their religions, and Slavery is the real and only religion of the South. To it other regions are evil in proportion to their freedom; other Free States are diabolical, more or less; Massachusetts is the Devil, because Antislavery is Antichrist.

Our reporters have told to horror-stricken ears the cruel excesses which succeeded the battle of Manasses. A young man from the North, we are told, finding a rebel soldier in a swoon, proffered his canteen: the Southerner drank, and revived; then immediately shot his benefactor. The story is intrinsically credible. Returning from his swoon, his first thought was for his cause, and the blow for that cause which he was on that field to strike! Supposing him even to have comprehended all, — to have recognized his preserver in his country's enemy, to have felt the gratitude which any brute must feel, — yet what business has he to let gratitude or any personal feeling come between him and his cause? That benefactor may be the very man to send a ball through Jeff. Davis's heart! He is not his own, else he could press that kindly hand: he is Slavery's; and Slavery has whispered all other spirits out of him, and filled him with its own. Ah, if Freedom but had champions so surcharged with her spirit! If she but had great lovers to match such haters!

Slavery is a god, and has in the South gradually created his own new heavens and new earth. In the latter generations, he has moulded the very brains in their wombs to his own image and likeness, so that they reek with hot blood when any foe speaks in unbelief of their creator. He is dear to them as to the eye is the light of which it is the organism.

Now, Northmen, with what do you confront this? Have you any Freedom-frenzy, with its superhuman strength? Do you worship Liberty with a passion such as the heart has for its blood? Is Liberty an uncompromisable principle to you, so that you count its foes the agents of the fiend upon earth? Has Boston treated Mr. Yancey, when there pleading for Slavery, as honestly and faithfully as Charleston treated Mr. Hoar, when there to distantly hint Liberty?

The other day, Mr. Speaker Grow, retiring temporarily from the chair of the House, called to that seat Mr. Burnett of Kentucky, an avowed sympathizer with treason. Some one called attention to the contrast between the Republican and the Southern Speaker, Orr, who never called any one to the chair but one of his own party; and evidently considered the contrast in Mr. Grow's favor! Trace the course of the two Speakers, and they will take you logically to the relative positions of the two armies on the evening of July 21; and until the country has got so far beyond these sentimentalities as not only to condemn utterly even so slight a dapperness as that of Mr. Grow, but to render it as impossible for Burnett to sit in Congress as it would be for John M. Botts to be in the Richmond Congress, it will put its trust in chariots and horsemen in vain. We are not in earnest for Freedom, as they are for Slavery: our battalions are not on the side of our God; theirs are thoroughly and utterly on the side of *their* God. Therefore we stand mystified and irritated, — eighteen millions held at bay and repulsed by eight!

At last, when it was too late, Napoleon had learned the deeper lesson; and he said, "No people devoted to its government and institutions can be conquered." *Devoted*, observe! It is the old word for victims bound on altars, and devoted to the gods; and Napoleon saw that men could be thus sacredly devoted to their freedom, thus laid on the altar of their country; and that, when they were so, something stronger than heavy artillery was at work. So, by his own authority, we must change the maxim, and read, "*The strongest battalions are those on the side of God.*"

Another lesson, and one following on this, is, that we must regard the forces in such a contest as this as more nearly equal than we are apt to assume. First, we must remember that a nation never attacks one of twice its population, unless in some way it has a full compensation for this discrepancy. In the present case, we know, that, when Sumter was attacked, the South was armed, the North unarmed: in the next place, the repossession of its lost integrity and wrested property made it necessary for the United States to take the attitude of an invader, and the real disabilities of fighting on an unfamiliar soil. Under the circumstances, it would have required an army at Manasses of two hundred thousand men to have made us equal in physical force to the Southern army there. Secondly, we are to remember that the very discrepancy in numbers and wealth between belligerents, whilst it often begets a dangerous sense of security in the stronger party, invariably leads the weaker to the fullest tension of every nerve and sinew, and the levying on every resource, however unusual. From these considerations, we see the plain natural causes for the seeming paradoxes to which attention has been called. We must more and more fix it in our minds, that *size* and *power* are by no means convertible terms or facts. A hornet is more than a match for a wolf. Emerson's epigram reminds us, —

> "Foxes are so cunning
> Because they are not strong."

In nature, weakness itself frequently becomes a source of strength: liability and danger make the eye quicker, the paw more velvety. Wild animals become more spiteful and deadly as they are smaller: the inhabitants of the tropics dread the roar of the lion less than the scent of the vinegar-bug. Already we have seen the law thus suggested borne out at the South in the effort to poison our troops; in the spying of important facts under flags of truce; in their confinement of the war, so far as they could, to the plan of the moccason, — picking off at night, ambuscade, masked battery, and the use of our own flag to protect themselves, and seduce our men into their trap.

When our army has fully learned its lessons, — moral and military, — the chaplain may preach on his text, "Manasseh is mine:" it will be ours in a more important sense than if our flag waved over it to-day.

XIV.

A REBELLION *vs.* A REVOLUTION.

THERE has been a general confusion in the minds of both parties as to their historical and moral position in this conflict. They of the South have claimed that they are revolutionists, and justify themselves under the right of revolution. Many of the North have accepted the terms; justly reasoning, that the right of revolution implies an interest, and possibly, as now, a duty pledged to prevent it. Revolution depends for its dignity and heroism purely upon the worth and justice of its cause; for, as all would applaud a child's resistance to his father when that father demanded of it some dishonorable act, so all would cry "Shame!" on the violent rebellion against a kind and good parent. Had our American Revolution been for the purpose of forming our Colonies into a band of robbers and pirates, no Pitt would have been found to plead our cause, no Lafayette to fight our battles. Revolution, in an unjust cause, is only an inauguration of bloodshed and assassination.

Therefore it is wrongly called Revolution. Revolution is a word nearly related to Evolution, and indicates the normal and healthy progression of the world on the prescribed orbit of civilization. Pangs it may have; but they are the previous pangs of birth into life. It may wring tears; but each tear falls in blessed light, and gives some tint to the bow that haloes the world. Revolution has marched on with the advancing world, and with it the fire of war and the cloud of sorrow; but its fire and cloud have been pillars leading on to Humanity's Promised Lands.

Those who have set themselves against these revolutions — the normal steps of human progression — have been always the Pharaohs, Hapsburgs, Philip the Seconds, George the Thirds, and Bombas; their use being always the negative one of making each advance more thorough by making it difficult and costly; their destiny, always to fail, in the end, to suppress the new germ. So, if this were a revolution in the South, this nation would now, ere its own majority is reached, be standing in the position of the hard Pharaoh and the Egyptian taskmasters towards the Israelitish bondmen, and actually in the same relation to the South that George the Third so lately held toward itself!

The South claims that this is the true attitude in which the parties stand, and bids us prepare for the fate that has ever overtaken the obstinate oppressor.

On the surface, and for the moment, the South is right in this. So long as the position of our Government is purely political, — so long as it remains, as now, a question of government against government, of authority against authority, — we are their obstinate George the Third; and *on that count* we are already partially, and in the end shall be completely, nonsuited.

But this defeat will be our real success; for it will

drive us from our present untenable fortress to that which the ages have reared for us, and whose guns command the continent and the world. RIGHT commands all trenches, even those of Liberty; and to it is assigned the power of silencing the batteries that defend the liberty of Wrong, under whatever mask of Independence it may hide. Men fighting for their "altars" are strong; but, if on those altars human victims lie bleeding, they are weaker than those *who come to rescue those victims.*

Behind the national army now in the field, there stands in the shadow another, silent and waiting. As yet, it is refused. Not until other defeats, and an exhaustion of other re-enforcements, will these re-enforcements be called on. They can calmly wait; for they are not three-years men: they are eternity men. The South already sees them behind there, more terrible than an army with banners: they desire to settle the war before this second army takes the sword. For they know that really the revolution is on our side, and that as soon as the nation feels that, and acts upon it, the strength of the South is gone. In that moment they become the Pharaohs and taskmasters, and America the revolutionary Israel, bursting their fetters, scorning their flesh-pots, and going forth in the strength of Israel's God to inherit the land declared unto their fathers.

WE ARE THE REVOLUTIONISTS. It was the revolution of the American nation that made this war necessary.

The South stands relatively where it always stood, and where the tyrant has stood since the world began. This is true, not in any fanciful or strained sense, but in the simplest and most direct sense. Slavery has always ruled this country. As soon as a seat of power was reared, Slavery assumed it. Its rod was extended over the lot of the righteous, and they put forth their hands to iniquity. It ruled commerce; it expunged the truth of history; it brought its Index Expurgatorius on the page of school-book and prayer-book. Scholars wrote for it; divines preached for it: it clasped the Bible with handcuffs, and festooned the Cross of Christ with chains.

Its tyranny was over the North. In the South was its throne: the Southerners were its royal family. On the North was laid its rod of iron. Under it their great men bowed low, licking the dust from the tyrant's foot, and getting in return his imperial kick. Did a minister plead for Liberty? Slavery commanded that he should be exiled from his pulpit, and his family live on a crust of bread. So it ordered, when Dudley Tyng "stood up for" the Christ of to-day with the scourges on his back, and sent a South-Carolinian to take his place in a Northern pulpit, to plot against the nation whilst in that pulpit. Did any senator speak for Freedom? He was avoided as a leper, or stricken down in his place. The North was made to plait the lashes for its own back, — to forge the chains for its own limbs: the men whom she furnished, and who were called Presidents and Representatives, were not Presidents nor Representatives, but minions and crawling courtiers, sitting under the footstool of Slavery. None could be trusted. Head after head even of the noblest was laid low, as if there were a dry-rot among men. The dog-star reigned and raged, and the best man could scarcely tell whether he would not be a slave-hound before night. We had no country. In proportion as we were real men, our country sank and hardened about us into a cold dungeon, where we lay chilled and chained, with vermin creeping over us.

Against this Tyrant, America at last inaugurated a revolution. Slowly and with many disparagements the feeble cause of Liberty prepared for a final struggle. Her pulses beat low; her heart-throbs are faint: she is only not crushed because purblind Oppression imagines the life already, or nearly, ebbed out. But an old fire, that was in deep alliance with the central heats of the earth, and under which old Wrong had again and again shrivelled like a burnt scroll, yet lingered in her heart. Anon the flame leapt out at eye and tongue; and despite the play of the engines, despite the cold-water jets sent from pulpit and press and society and office, the winds of heaven fanned that flame until the parties were consumed, the political elements melted with fervent heat, and Slavery compelled to begin the world over again, and rebuild its throne over those ashes if it could!

It was the noblest revolution the world ever saw that

placed Abraham Lincoln in the White House at Washington; the noblest, because the first ever known upon this planet where the legitimate weapons of Truth were alone used. These mighty strongholds yielded to the voices, the persuasions, the reasons, of earnest and just men: they were besieged with arrows of light, shelled with the bombs of Free School and Free Thought. "Love is the hell-spark that burneth up the mountain of Iniquity," said Mohammed. So also have we found it. Besides those who truckled to Slavery with mean motives, there were many fond and simple souls, who could "think no evil," were it of the Devil; and these yielded to Slavery that vast extent of rope, wherewith, when attained, rogues do proverbially hang themselves. And thus the revolution, without the firing of a gun from the side of the revolutionists, had gone on, until the steps of Freedom were on the threshold of a liberated and redeemed New World. The dayspring from on high had already visited us: the banner which had fallen out of the sky to blazon itself only in the scars and stripes on the slave's back, or on some weaker nation beside us, once more floated up, and promised to symbolize, as of old, the streaks of Humanity's advancing day.

The Southern movement is, then, not a revolution, but a rebellion against the noblest of revolutions. It is a league of confederates against the peaceful and legal evolution of Liberty on this continent. It is an Insurrection against a Resurrection. It is Slavery, hoary tyrant of the ages, standing before Humanity's morning, lifting its bars against the day-streaks, and crying, "Back, back, accursed Dawn, into the chambers of Night!"

The instinct of slaveholders has probed this matter very accurately. They know that sunrise respects not the protest of owl and bat against it. They have discovered that the North Star is a kind of Ossawattomie star; refusing to stop its light at Mason and Dixon's line; sending its incendiary ray far down into cane-brake and dismal swamp; finding many a poor fugitive to hold with its glittering eye until he is safe in the land of Freedom. They know that the sunlight will not respect the sacred soil, and that their only hope is in seeing that it shall shine through "bars." They scarcely rebelled in time: they will have hard work building the northward wall of their fortress in time to resist the arrows of Phœbus. But they are doing their best.

It is a great mistake, however, for us to suppose that they wish to subjugate the North. They have no desire to cast themselves straight across the railroad where the train of Civilization must pass. It is true that all they desire is to be let alone. But what does it imply to let them alone? It implies that a nation which has heard at the door of its sepulchre the divine mandate, "Come forth!" and whose hands and feet and face are already half divested of their grave-clothes, shall sink back again to decay, take again the napkin about its face, surrender its tissues again to the worm. There is not one healthy movement of a free nation, not one word or step, however innocent and unconscious, which can by any possibility let Slavery alone. Slavery knows they cannot, if it is united with them in one nation: it would discover, if separated, that Civilization is no red-tapist; and that free America cannot let oppression in the South alone, more than it can let it alone in the Old World. Plutarch tells us that Bessus, the Pæonian, destroyed a nest of sparrows with cruelty; and, being reproached with this wantonness, replied, that he destroyed them justly, since they constantly reproached him untruthfully with the murder of his father. Thus he disclosed his crime. What the twittering of innocent sparrows was to the parricide, such must for ever be the natural influences of Liberty — its free schools, its free speech, its material progress — to parricidal Wrong the world over. Let us not wonder if the tyrannies of the Old World smile complacently at the attempt of the Southern Bessus to destroy the brood of Liberty in America. Freedom will never let them alone; will never cease to accuse them; will for ever proclaim from the house-top the crimes they have committed in the cellars and closets.

When Lieut. Maury came down from the dome of the United-States Observatory, where for so many years he had watched the stars to so little purpose, — never having discovered how they in their courses for ever "fight against Sisera," — to bend all he had learned there to the behest of Slavery, the first evidence the country had of his treachery was that the light-houses all along the coast were darkened. It was well. 'Tis an exact symbol of what the Confederacy to which he had attached himself means. To quench all the lights which guide Humanity; to darken every guiding beacon to which the voyagers in the ancient Night are looking; to extinguish every hope lit up on the shores of the Future, — that is their design. "Darken the light-houses!" cry the wreckers of Humanity. "Let no ray shine out upon the night of Oppression! Let the brave ships with their immortal freightage be dashed upon the breakers! for so alone can their treasures gild the coast of Slavery."

Shall we now spend our blood, our time, our strength, fighting with Slavery for the treasures dragged from the waves, — wrecker against wrecker? In that they will be ahead of us: their drags and nets of spoil are longer and better, their eagerness for their prey greater. Shall we rekindle those extinguished light-houses? Shall we see, that, all along the Atlantic and the Pacific and the Gulf, the rays of Freedom and Justice to all shine out clear and beautiful, marking for every struggling bark — for Germany, Hungary, Poland, for all — a path of light to a haven of safety and rest? Then we save the wrecker and the wrecked. We kindle lights that shine not only outward upon those ready to perish in the stormy waves of Old-World oppression, but inward upon our more pitiable fellowmen, wandering in the darkness of crime, morally wrecked on the rocks of Barbarism, because America has hitherto failed to provide with the beacons of trade and power those of national righteousness and honor.

Thus, and thus alone, we cease to be in the seat of George the Third, fighting against the bud that by normal growth would grow from our side and climb to its fruit. We ourselves become revolutionists against our own wrong. We emerge from the ancient kingdom of Oppression, and make this a holy war, — a second Revolution, achieving for the nations of the world more than our first achieved for thirteen Colonies.

XV.

EXCALIBUR.

The centuries as they roll bring no season without its fresh laurel for the brow of King Arthur. The sun never rises and sets, but it leaves some new gleam of light on the jewelled hilt, on the fine-tempered blade, of Excalibur, — sword of Arthur, "flower of kings."

There came a day when out of the boiling sea a great hand emerged, holding out this sword, with an inscription which declared its name, and its power, if wielded by its true king, to cut through iron or steel, or conquer the strongest foe. It was given to Arthur;

for was not he its true king, who stood for justice, for honor, for the cause of the weak and wronged?

The virtue of the sword, as its name indicates, lay in its Calibre. It was no larger than other swords; *but its quality was finer.* Character is more than size; and the sword that defends the innocent and the wronged must, in the end, win the day. So, in the hand of Arthur, Excalibur never failed.

At length, the noble King Arthur drew near his end. Then went he, with one of his knights, near to the sea, and Excalibur was cast therein: again the great white hand emerged, and caught the sword. The legend runs, that soon afterward the king himself was borne away to some happy isle by nymphs. But he never died; and the prophecies remained, that, when his race — *our race* — shall be worthy to receive him, King Arthur the Imperishable shall return, bringing with him Excalibur the Unconquerable.

All along the line of our army, — from the Chesapeake to the Missouri, — many eyes have strained to meet one like thine, O Arthur! flower of kings. We have watched night and day, if through the dust and smoke of any conflict we could see the trusty Excalibur flashing in the light. It is not there: so we gain or lose as the fortune of war may decide. With Excalibur there is no chance, but certainty.

When we are worthy to receive him; when we stand true Knights of Humanity; when we have set our hearts to strike for the innocent and wronged; when we have bound ourselves by a holy compact, as a Legion of Honor, to strike down those who raise themselves upon the weak, — then the royal Soul of our race shall rise, and return to lead us; and the sword that never failed shall carve the path of our victory through every "bar," and bring back the thirty-two stars as jewels in its hilt.

As yet, the watchers must sit by the foaming, seething sea of events, awaiting the great hand, and the sword which alone can win the day for America. Not yet, not yet. As yet, our leaders turn their faces from the hunted fugitive, even if forced to receive him; as yet, the soldier's sword has not the calibre to carve the iron of the slave's manacle. When our Anglo-Saxon blood mounts to its royal height, and grasps its final, noblest weapon, four million chains will fall; nay, six million hearts, whose drugged blood owns the same fountain with ours, will cast off the virus which has maddened them, and every State hasten as a Knight to the Table where Arthur reigns.

Why does not this nation at once draw this sword? Why does it not, owning what is whispered in every heart, that this war means *freedom for all or chains for all*, at once inscribe "EMANCIPATION" on its banner?

No one questions that Slavery is the cause of this Rebellion.

No one questions that to recover the Union as it was — i.e., with Slavery in it — is to recover the elements that have led to this collision, and must bring it on again whenever the Slave interest thinks itself strong enough for another effort.

No one questions but that the only alternative of this will be the subjugation of the North in a moral sense, — the suspension over the ballot-box of the hair-strung sword of civil war; so that fear, and not conviction, shall decide every election.

No one questions that Slavery is the one stain and blot which disgraces our flag, and cripples our progress; and that, but for the absence of any power to exterminate it in the Constitution, the nation should and would have abolished it for ever.

No one questions, that, by the appeal which Slavery has made to an arbitrament beside the Constitution, compelling the temporary obedience to military law and military necessity, by which the Constitution itself has provided for its own possible suspension, our nation has a right to strike at the very root of the evil, which, so long as it remained subject to the Constitution, it must tolerate.

No one questions the position of John Quincy Adams, that the power to abolish Slavery is contained in the war-power.

Yet, in this war, law has been as often suspended in favor of Slavery as against it: for it is a direct violation of law for one of our soldiers or military officers to return a fugitive slave; such return being provided for in due form of law, and assigned to appointed civil officers. Where, by the growing compulsion of events, our Government has been compelled to retain slaves, it has done so with all the tenderness for the South that a mother might show for her pet babe. To-day comes the news, that, by a final decision, escaping slaves shall be retained, whether belonging to loyal or disloyal; but, as if frightened at reaching this dizzy height of resolution, the order of the Secretary of War immediately provides, that any slave, wishing to return to the service from which he has escaped, shall have no let or hinderance! We quote this, not as an instance of unfaithfulness to Freedom, but as an example of the infatuation and terror which seem to seize upon and confuse all our public men when they touch this question of property in man. Any one whose wits are about him can see, that, by this order, any treacherous Negro of Governor Letcher's household may be bribed into escaping to Fortress Monroe, and, after suitable observations, "voluntarily return," to give such information, as, at Manasses, the rebels had, by their own account, to pay a hundred thousand dollars for.

Why this timidity? Why this overweening tenderness with human bondage? One would suppose that a system repulsive to all the instincts of Humanity, which can exist only by a toleration almost barbaric, would be at once crushed when it became an outlaw and a foe; but here we are pirouetting amongst its interests as daintily as Mignon among the eggs she dares not break. Wherefore?

Not because any member of this Administration loves Slavery, but because the Government fears to divide its physical forces; that is, to alienate certain persons in the North and (supposed) in the South from the cause of the Union itself, as separate from the Slavery question: in fact, *for the sake of certain persons, who, in case of a direct issue between the American Union and Slavery, would take sides with Slavery.*

But if such men should, unwashed, put forth their hands to defend the Union, would it not be a sure proof that it would be the old tar-and-feather Union, — a Union not fit to be saved?

Unto their assembly, mine honor, be not thou united!

Indeed it is, in the eyes of every lover of universal Freedom, the highest mission of this conflict to liberate this land from the influence of that vile Northern Mephistopheles, — the party which has in every way fostered the arrogance of Slavery, and encouraged the madness of the South; which it is now forced to abandon in the conflict to which it has seduced that misguided section. The guilt of this Rebellion is not heaviest on Dixie's Land, by any means.

These Tories would be a drag and a curse to our side, if they should espouse it. The hearts of freemen the world over would shrink back chilled and distrustful.

"We shall march conquering, — not through their presence;
Songs shall inspirit us, — not from their lyre;
Deeds shall be done, — whilst they boast their quiescence,
Still bidding crouch, whom the rest bade aspire."

XVI.

A FELICITATION.

In the pecuniary crisis of 1857, Stackpole, on hearing that a certain bank had gone under, exclaimed, "Bully for that bank!" His astonished auditors asked why his admiration was elicited for a bank that had just broken. "Broke!" exclaimed Stackpole, amazed at their stupidity: "well, why shouldn't it break? What else were banks made for? But see how long it held out, — fourteen days! *That's* what I call a bully bank!"

Perhaps, on the same principle, we should say, "Bully for the Democratic party!" Of course, we expected it to go for the South, in the end. What else was it meant for? We were scarcely so green as to expect that Slavery's Northern factotum would ever seriously pass through a crisis involving a cessation, even temporary, of such stated religious services as the abuse of the North and glowing eulogy of the South, to say nothing of having such a means of grace as hunting fugitive Humanity for our Southern brethren disturbed by the "contraband" neology, without breaking down. We had, from the first, prepared our ears to hear a chorus of somewhat cracked voices singing the plaintive melody, "Carry me back!" This was *en règle*. It was what the metaphysicians call the "structural and normal development of its central idea."

But, on the whole, we feel a disposition to be duly thankful at the result. It cannot be denied that the party held out pretty well. It has failed at last, but not without losing many of its most talented leaders, and being fearfully decimated in numbers. It has not even enjoyed the delight of coming out in an open licking of its quondam master's hand. "Hypocrisy," says the French satirist, "is the homage that vice pays to virtue." The South is too shrewd not to see that the *quasi* support of this Government, under which the party conventions have found it necessary to conceal the poison they would administer, is an attestation of the true temper of the masses they hope to control,— the homage that disloyalty finds it necessary to pay to the throned patriotism of the people.

There is really no cause for apprehending any evil from these sitters on the fence. In due time, as we have said, the fence will be so sharp, that those who try it will be cut in two. But meanwhile it may be held as a general truth, that those who have not the courage to take a stand on either side will scarcely have courage or strength to help our cause, if they should adopt it. On looking over the early chronicles of our first Revolution, we find that our earnest and patriotic fathers had to contend with a vast deal more of disloyalty than we have now. The historians give us evidence, that, even so late as after the destruction of tea in Boston Harbor, a man might have been roughly handled in Boston who should have advocated a complete separation from England. It was some time after the battle of Bunker Hill that this separation became an avowed object of the war. More people in this country are now to be found who advocate a complete casting-off of the yoke of Slavery, than, at the same stage of the first Revolution, were in favor of casting off the yoke of England; and just in the proportion, that, under the tuition of events, our country then rose to greater earnestness and bolder steps, the number of sycophant Tories increased all over the country. Some of the most fearful scenes of bloodshed occurred between the Revolutionists and the Tories.

Now see how much better off we are. Val. and Breck. are protected in Washington by their very insignificance. The Tory Conventions, with all their pusillanimous talk, are to-day regarded, by the best men of the party they claim to represent, as only the hanging-out of crape upon its door, to indicate that the pulses of the living no longer beat through its veins.

There is one — and only one — way in which these Northern Tories and dapper neutrals can work us an injury; and that is by being regarded by our Government at Washington as a party worthy to be considered in any of its measures, or of any effort at its conciliation. Let our Government have no Mrs. Grundy after whose opinions to inquire in the solemn emergency. Let it be brave and earnest, knowing that the great heart of the people moves with it; knowing, too, that, in these high magnetic conditions, the people see very shrewdly into affairs. It is through inattention or indifference that they are usually hoodwinked by politicians: now they are neither inattentive nor indifferent; and the demagogues will soon find that it is they who are hoodwinked in thinking so. We have no fear whatever of the verdict that the people will pass upon the contemptible and selfish determination of these men to decline all exertion to save the temple of Liberty from the flames that threatened to envelop it, and sit down to boil their party-pots in the fire.

XVII.

TO THE PRESIDENT OF THE UNITED STATES.

HONORED SIR: —

From the many conflicting and vague statements with which the telegraph fills the air, one seems to have obtained the clearness and authenticity of a fact; this, namely, — that GARIBALDI, the patriot whose knightly kiss broke the evil spell which bound the Sleeping Beauty of the Mediterranean, whose sword has carved a gateway through the age-hardened prison-walls of Italy, has sent word to America, "*If this war is for Freedom, I come with twenty thousand men.*"

Garibaldi, sir, is a symbol. The spirit of this age has produced him; and millions in every land recognize in him the appearance in our age of the Forerunner, — the Voice in the Wilderness that has never failed any age, and that cries now, as of old, "Prepare ye the way of the Lord: make his paths straight. And now also the axe is laid to the root of the tree: every tree that bringeth not forth good fruit is hewn down, and cast into the fire."

There are also in our midst other symbols. Never was there a Moses without his Pharaoh; never a John without his Herod. We have a party that has gained a certain fictitious strength by Wrong and Deceit; and their leaders say, "*As soon as this is a war for Freedom, we leave you, taking our twenty thousand men.*"

Between these two symbols you are compelled to choose, — Garibaldi and millions of Garibaldini all over the world, who can draw no sword but for Justice and Liberty, on the one hand; and, on the other, the Pro-slavery politicians, who hate Liberty more than all else, and whose half-hearted, muttering support to this Government is given only in the ratio of that Government's servility to Slavery. As Garibaldi is only known as the hero of European Liberty, so are Vallandigham, Richmond, & Co. known only for the extent to which they have crawled on their bellies before Slavery, and the malignancy with which they have sought to wound the heel of Humanity. To accept one of these parties is to refuse the other.

The American people look on very anxiously to see to which of these you will turn, and which you will consequently make up your mind to alienate. This much any one may say for the American people. Further than this, each one can speak only for himself; and since, by the nature of our institutions, the responsibility for what is done by our Government must be shared to some extent by the humblest individual, it becomes the solemn duty of every man, who has an earnest conviction, to utter it, — as it is of every man, who can strike a blow for his country, to strike it.

Now, therefore, I, sir, the writer of these pages, who have seen my native State, the natural garden-spot of this country, withered and wasted by Slavery; who have seen its race of honorable and upright men disappear before a population of pygmies; who, exiled to the North, have seen there how a nation can turn from its great birthright to be warped and ruined by receiving into its system a great moral poison, sugared over by an important interest, — have seen there the best and bravest men alienated from, and enlisted against, a country in which they found no place unless their most sacred convictions were laid down at the threshold, whilst the only titles to places of trust or power were supple knee-joints and pliant vertebration; and who, having known these things, arose one blessed morning, and, invoking the benison of Heaven on a bit of paper which bore the name of Abraham Lincoln, cast then my first vote, hoping that it might be for the liberation of this country from a great and dwarfing crime, — do now implore the President to accept the proffer of

Giuseppo Garibaldi, and thereby proclaim to the world that this country links its destiny with that of Universal Freedom.

The only test of our good faith in this is, that the world shall at once see inscribed on our banner, "IMMEDIATE AND UNCONDITIONAL EMANCIPATION."

1. It is legal. Your Excellency is sworn to execute the laws: therefore you cannot even consider a measure that is violative of the Constitution and laws. The Constitution and laws, in providing for possible war, do, in case of war, at once deliver up the Government to the laws of war; so that to follow the letter of the Constitution in times of war, when military law and advantage demanded the contrary, would be violating the Constitution. There are times when the Constitution can only be obeyed by its temporary suspension at the command of the universal and necessary code, which, in common with the organic law of all nations, it recognizes. The suspension of the Habeas Corpus, and the discussion which followed it, have made it perfectly clear to the people, that, in each case where it was suspended, it would have been unconstitutional to follow the ordinary provision of the Constitution. It needs no discussion to prove that the same laws, which take from a traitor the ordinary form and process of law, may deprive an institution, that proves traitorous and deadly to the country, of its ordinary guaranties. It thus becomes simply a question of whether Slavery stands in this attitude towards the country.

2. It is just. The South would destroy the Union, in the interest of Slavery. The Nation must destroy Slavery, in the interest of the Union.

In the interest of Slavery, the territorial integrity of the country has been destroyed, and some arms, forts, and money seized. Is that all? If so, perhaps the account between this Nation and Slavery might be settled by the repentance of Slavery, and a return of the stolen articles.

But it is less than a centime of the account which this nation holds against Slavery. Years of usurpation and corruption; of insults and abuses heaped upon Freedom, in whatever form it tried to maintain its slight foothold on the continent; years now summed up, and culminant in a frantic civil-war, involving the daily expenditure of millions, the perversion of the means and powers of the people, the suspension and lasting injury of trade, the re-instating of piracy on the high seas; more than all, the death of vast numbers of the youth of America, and the darkening of tens of thousands of hitherto happy homes, — all these are in the account that this nation has now to settle with Slavery. Can they be repaid by the conquest of what forces the South can bring into the field? Will it be enough if Slavery should at length agree to ground its arms until it is stronger? Can it be settled by a truce of one or two or ten years? Is the balance struck, if we have the old Union, with the old causes at work in it, to bring forth like results in the future?

Justice can be satisfied in that alone which satisfies Wisdom, — THE UTTER DESTRUCTION OF SLAVERY. In no other way can we act up to the lessons which Slavery has taught us of its own blasting nature; in no other way can we, as a nation, obtain that blessing for which we have already paid the full price in treasure and blood, — the riddance from the accursed evil under which we have groaned ever since we became a nation.

This is justice to ourselves. I have not mentioned that higher justice which is due to four millions of human beings, cruelly deprived of "the right to life, liberty, and the pursuit of happiness," which our nation, in the pure aspirations of its youth, meant to secure for all. You are bound to stand by legal formulas. Yet I cannot forget what I once heard you say, with luminous words, that seemed to shine out like responses to the everlasting stars that then and there gleamed above you: "Every man that comes into the world has a mouth to be fed, and a back to be clothed. By a notable coincidence, each has also two hands. Now, I take it that those hands were meant to feed that mouth, and clothe that back; and any institution that deprives them of that right, and the rights deducible from it, strikes at the very roots of natural justice, which is also political wisdom."

I pray you, Mr. President, to remember, that, when the laws of war permit you to restore millions to those natural rights, every day thereafter that they remain deprived of them will be traceable to your own door!

3. It is merciful. Not only merciful to the slave, that he should have this cruel and galling yoke that binds him to the plane of the brute removed; not only merciful to us, that the heart-burnings and animosities which have rent our land should be laid by the eradication of their cause; not only merciful to posterity, that this fearful and irrepressible source of trouble and guilt should not be bequeathed to them; but, more than to these or to all others, a decree of emancipation would be MERCIFUL TO THE SOUTH.

Up from broad and beautiful plains, worn out and desolate; from undrained marshes and swamps, whose very wealth has turned to malaria; from the locked treasures of gold and iron in Virginia and the Carolinas; from the eighty-five thousand white adults in Virginia who cannot read or write, and the even more fearful proportions of ignorance in more Southern States; from the young men trained to licentiousness and idleness, whose remnant of strength is to-day given to the monster which has ruined them; from the tearful, anxious eyes of mothers, wives, sisters, whose souls know the agony of seeing the son, brother, and husband the easy prey of the temptations that cannot be escaped,—oh! from all these, sir, would come a response to your decree for Liberty: "Merciful, most merciful!"

There is a weak love that yields and indulges; there is a great and divine love that spares not to smite when to smite is best,—ever giving what is wanted more than what is wished. An old legend relates that in the

court of King Arthur was a poor dwarf, named Carl. He was much pitied by the king and his court, and there were stern orders that none should harm the poor dwarf. It was also supposed that Carl's mind was defective; for he every day went about the court with a sword, beseeching each knight to cut off his head with it. The knights, of course, would refuse to slay the dwarf, who, they supposed, wished thus to be relieved of life. At length, on a day, the dwarf stood before Sir Gawain, and with a voice full of earnest appeal, and with tears in his eyes, said, "Gawain, canst thou not love me enough to smite off my head with this sword?" Sir Gawain was so moved by this, that, in an instant, he seized the sword, and cut off the poor dwarf's head.

Poor dwarf no longer! The evil spell which had bound him in his misshapen form, until one of Arthur's knights should cut off his head, was now broken, and, in noble and knightly form and guise, Sir Carleton stood where poor Carl was before.

Ah, 'tis a great, a godlike mercy which can smite its object!

And there are dwarfs upon earth, from age to age, that only thus can have the evil spell broken, and rise to their full stature. Sometimes these dwarfs are States.

4. There is no real obstacle or danger in the way of it. I know there are seeming lions in the path; but several pilgrim nations have gone that way, and found

the lions chained each side, and impotent. We have been told that dreadful scenes and vindictive actions follow emancipation; that the Negroes will not labor but as slaves, and thus become idlers on a nation's hands. The facts bear otherwise.

There is yet to be shown the State, that emancipated its slaves, which did not at once rise above the stature into which it was before dwarfed.

It has yet to be shown that Right has ever wronged any.

If, under the formidable circumstances which now surround our nation, we should fear the expenses or the labors attending such a step, mark how Haiti stands ready to bear a hand to the holy work. The Queen of the Antilles sits there with her ungathered wealth about her, her spices and fruits gilding every wave around her shores, awaiting the ten millions of gatherers to whom she can yet give a hospitable home. One word from you, sir, and she is a recognized sister Republic. Another word, and, whilst African troops march on to see that your decree is executed, the aged, the women and children, which we can scarcely sustain, are borne away to the happy clime where no fevers nor lashes await them.

5. It is the only path to a real success. We justly count as a great natural fortress against Secession that mountain range stretching from Pennsylvania almost to the Gulf, — whose brave and hardy inhabitants have justified Milton's designation of Freedom as "a mountain

nymph:" why should we overlook the millions of the oppressed stretching into every branch and twig of Southern society, who, by the laws of God, are our natural allies, unless, by our inhumanity, we drive them to the side of the enemy? Is it best to have seven hundred thousand fighting men of the South our enemies, when we can make them our friends? We have certain knowledge that we have been represented to that class as their bitterest foes: they have been told that our plan was to slay a proportion of them, and banish the rest. This falsehood has been systematically and carefully circulated throughout the cabins and plantations, and justified by the most religious Southerners as a necessity of defence. We have done nothing to disabuse the slave's mind in this particular. Consequently, although here and there a knowing Negro has been able to do this for us, the mass has been deceived, and is working most devotedly against us.

At this rate, we shall be defeated, and, as I think, deservedly.

But this war must, as now conducted, prove more and more a disheartening one to our people and our soldiers.

As at Manasses our men conquered one battery, only to find two more opening upon that, we all have a misgiving that a victory over the South would lead to the most painful complications. We must hold on to our victory after we have got it; for it will have a perpetual tendency to elude us. It was, you remember, a difficult problem to decide, whether the wolf, or the man who, having caught him, had to hold him fast, was made captive by the exploit. If the cause of the hatred of the South to the North and the nation and to free government were removed, their rage against these would still remain in the breast of the present Southern generation; but for a generation we could hold them quiet. The hatred might even be transmitted to the next generation: that, too, might be held. But in this age, as we see in the case of France and England, feuds must gradually be worn away before advancing commercial and other interests; and, with the root of Disunion plucked up, the third generation at the South, and perhaps the next, would thank us for the painful surgery with which we saved them, and we should be bound together by all natural ties, — ties which Slavery alone holds in abeyance now. If this fair prospect were ahead, our people would forget in its glory the pains and deprivations of the present, and go forward animated by that faith which is the substance of things hoped for.

Moreover, the many disheartening circumstances that press upon us now would be removed. To the soldier, applause is sweet. But we have heard no plaudits from the world looking on, — none from England or France or Germany or Italy. They cried "*Brava!*" to America, when our ballots bore you, sir, to the Capitol: they are silent now that our bayonets would defend your right there. We hear from over the seas only cold calculations of the probable issue. The civilized world stands ready with an equal welcome to either party that succeeds. These cold buckets, which are cast upon a conflict so sacred to us, we have invited, by placing the issue on the lowest plane of which it was susceptible.

But this could not be, if, in the face of the world, we rose to the standard of right and civilization which those very nations have uplifted, and up to which even Russia has come before us. We ourselves have from the first held — hold now — the power to decide the posture of every foreign nation toward this Rebellion. Apart from Slavery, England can only see in the Southern movement the presentation to our own lips of the chalice we once offered hers. In this she is right. We are wrong and presumptuous in any complaint. But the civilized world is antislavery; and if, in this war, we did but touch the hem of Liberty's vesture, we should be thrilled with an inspiration and sympathy which would soon make us every whit whole. We should come in contact with that electric belt which binds the hearts of freemen round the world; and up from every nation and clime would swell the *vivas* and *bravas* and *hurrahs* which would make our every soldier thrice a soldier, and cheer us on to a victory which every eye would see already written in the book of Fate.

6. It is thus alone that your Excellency can be faithful to your parole of honor to the United States. You have nobly discerned that your oath of office required

you to preserve the Union and the Constitution at any cost. You can hardly fail to remember that the American people, in electing you over candidates representing all varieties of opinion, declared that certain principles should prevail in the Government of this country,—principles to which you had pledged your allegiance. When afterward the alternatives of this painful conflict, or the abandonment of the principles on which you were elected, were again and again presented to the American people, they again and again refused any and every compromise of those principles, whatever the result might be. You cannot be true to them, if you compromise them, or fail to defend them. *Slavery would now wrest more than half of this country from its allegiance to those principles.* Either the Principle which placed you in office, or the Institution which is in deadly grip with it, must fall to the ground.

Remember, sir, that the people did not place you in office to preserve the Union merely: *that* they had under Fillmore and Buchanan and Pierce; and they might have retained it by electing Breckinridge instead of yourself. But, not doing so, they declared that the Union should be administered in the interest of Freedom, even more than in the interest of peace and conciliation. To that end your honor stands plighted. If any peace shall come in which that end is lost, the country is defeated, whatever victory its military arm may have achieved.

Can you, sir, preserve the United States with Slavery

therein? Will Slavery ever be united with the principles you represent? Is not the effort to make it so akin to the effort at any chemic impossibility,—as the union exclusively of fire and water, of oil and alcohol?

It is not by presenting to the country its old hulls, riveted with steel or welded with fire together, that you can fulfil your trust. It is not by returning us a Union in which it will be virtually impossible ever to elect another Republican President, for fear of another insurrection. That would be to restore us a country bound hand and foot. If Freedom can alone be free by the destruction of Slavery, you cannot, in honor, flinch from signing the death-warrant of that system.

In the ancient Promethean games, each racer bore in his hand a lighted torch. The one who first reached the goal, *with his torch still lighted*, won the prize. If he came in foremost, but with torch extinguished, the later comer, who came in with lighted torch, was declared victor.

No victory in this war can be a victory to America, which does not bring in, bright and burning, the torch of Liberty,—ay, of African Liberty, as far as the people by their last election declared that they could and would control and limit it,—which the Nation gave you, lighted, to bear in their van. And, if Slavery has resolved to stake its life on the wresting of rights which the people have irrevocably denied it, either that life or the verdict of the nation must be sacrificed. *Which shall it be?* The people decided the question when they accepted a war with the South rather than a denial of their principles; and to it, unless their rulers debauch them, they will stand. We claim of you that you shall fulfil Frederick the Great's definition of a prince as "the first of subjects," and prove it by being the last to yield the standard which they have lifted, and of which you are the symbol.

By proclaiming Freedom to all, white or black, who will rally to the defence of our imperilled banner, you are told that you will make enemies to yourself and the cause of the nation. You may, sir, make of secret enemies open ones. The serpent that now creeps in the grass may think it safe to come into the path; but that will be a benefit. It would be not the least good of recognizing a direct issue with Slavery, that it would be a better detective than Vidocq of the secret traitors, who, whilst sentimentalizing about the Union, really hold it as secondary and subservient to Slavery, and only refrain from mutiny on the Ship of State because they hope to make it a slaver before the voyage is over.

But, sir, when the half-hearted go, the whole-hearted arrive. The Albany and Columbus cliques are a cheap price to pay for the Garibaldis with their twenty thousands.

There is, honored sir, a class of men in this country but little known, — men who have been kept out of the politics and parties by which the forces of a country are usually gauged, because of an enthusiasm for Liberty and a hatred of Slavery, as intense and devoted as the enthusiasm for Slavery and the hatred of Freedom which the South is showing. They are men who have sacrificed the fair prospects of life, the wealth and power which usually absorb men, for a truer devotion to the cause of the weak and degraded, even against the nation when it was wrong. They are men who hold their lives at the beck and call of Justice. They stand to-day hand on hilt, and await the one word at which their swords flash out.

That word is EMANCIPATION.

These are not men that require to be waked up, nor do they need a long drill: they have long been wide awake, and they were born drilled. Only let that countersign, which Nature wrote on their hearts when they came into the world, be uttered, and you shall see again the Scourges of God, the Avengers, the Men of Destiny, — men born to conquer Slavery, as is the eagle to destroy the serpent that coils about its nest, — sweeping downward from every plain and hill, riding on every wind, until Humanity is avenged, the Tyrant and his host overthrown, and Peace bends once more her blue vault over a happy land, unflecked by a cloud of wrong, glorious with the sun-burst of impartial Freedom.

But, sir, besides this resource, upon which you have not drawn, even if you know of its existence, — a resource upon which only the Liberty which includes the slave can draw, — I believe you would find that the people are generally prepared for this measure.

The very appearances of division and disloyalty in the North, which may intimidate our leaders, may well be considered indications of a growing and bolder feeling among the masses. The appearance of activity amongst the compromisers is an indication of an increasing exasperation amongst the people against this Rebellion, and a deepening conviction that a blow at the cause of it is necessary. The uprising of one sentiment is always attended by the excitation of its antagonist.

War is a swift and infallible educator. The old mansion yet stands at Perth Amboy, where, in the midst of the American Revolution, the British Howe, having called for a conference with the Americans, met John Adams, Benjamin Franklin, and Edward Rutledge, and proposed to them a grant from England of relief from the taxes under which they had groaned, and a full amnesty, if they would lay down their arms. How they would have leapt at the offer a little before! At Concord, at Lexington, every American musket would have fallen to the ground before such a proposition.

Bunker Hill came: we were defeated there.

But there stands the monument of which every American is justly most proud, though it stands on the field where we were defeated; *for there the gate of compromise with the oppressor closed for ever.*

When our fathers began their Revolution, it was against an unjust tax. Its removal would have closed the matter at once. After a few months of war, its removal and many other privileges are offered; but the war has unsealed a higher aim. To the compromise proposition, our fathers replied, "No: THIS WAR ENDS ONLY WITH THE ENTIRE INDEPENDENCE OF AMERICA."

I think, sir, that, even at this stage of our second revolution against an internal tyrant, the concession of an amnesty to Slavery on condition of its grounding arms would be with difficulty obtained from the people; and that the indignation which a few weeks ago would have been allayed by the return of forts, and call for a convention on the part of the South, rises each day, and cannot now be restrained from the natural climax that will sweep the source of all our evils and discords out of our land for ever.

Thus, and thus alone, can we have an enduring peace. Short of this, it is difficult to see even in a victory any thing but an armistice which shall be the armistice of a generation of cowards, evading a task because it is hard, by adjourning one thrice as hard for their children.

Sir, 'tis not often in this world that to one man is given the magnificent opportunity which the madness of a great wrong has placed within your reach.

For the first time, there stands a man in the Earth empowered to break four millions of fetters from the hands, minds, and hearts of immortal beings.

What prophetic tongue can tell of the plaudits that reach far into the procession of the ages, or of the free glad voices which shall deliver from generation to generation the name and the story of the lowly youth,— the honest laborer,— the President who uplifted a race from the dungeon of Slavery, and cleared a nation's path straight to its sublime destiny?

But, ah! see what a precipice stretches downward from this sunlit summit! Far happier the rude boy, with his axe, unnamed, than one on whom Earth's millions of eyes shall turn, only to remember that he could have saved mankind, but faltered and failed.

Woe to him to whom four millions of slaves shall point their shackled hands, and say, "There is just the one man, whom, out of Earth's millions, God elected as him who should have power to remove our yokes, to raise us from beasts of burden to men; unsealing for us the fountains of affection, hope, aspiration, which the Father has provided as living water for his weary children. He swooned on the great moment.

'Blot out his name, then; record one lost soul more,
One task more declined, one more footpath untrod,
One more triumph for devils, and sorrow for angels;
One wrong more to man, one more insult to God.'"

Woe to him whom posterity, reaping its bitter harvest of agitation and affliction from the dire root of all our evils, shall remember only to curse as the one who, alone of all men in the history of this nation, stood on the moment and the spot where it was legal and practicable to pluck up the roots of the infernal tree, but who failed to put forth his hand.

Mr. President, History stands with the blank scroll before her: her pen she holds ready; the next word you must dictate. Shall it be Slavery or Freedom?

XVIII.

TO THE AMERICAN PEOPLE.

Old legends state, that once, in the midst of the city of Rome, a vast and fearful chasm opened. The people fled in terror to their Oracles, which said, "When that which is in Rome is most precious shall be cast therein, the chasm will be closed."

Then did each Roman — old and young, man and maid — bring of their treasures the richest, and cast therein; but yet the abyss yawned wider and wider in the city's heart.

At length, a young man rose before the council, and said, "Romans, what is it that Rome holds most precious? Is it not her Manhood?" Thus saying, he leaped into the chasm, and it closed above him for ever.

It is not all fable. In every nation, the abyss has at some time yawned, and closed only by the sacrifice of manhood.

Under the heart of America, it opens to-day. We began by casting in this and that treasure. One brought his compromise, another his diplomacy, another his military fame: still the abyss closed not.

Is there not, then, in America any thing precious enough to close it? My brothers, it is not the order of this universe that an emergency should come to brute or man or nation for which — if to pass it be lawful — the strength has not been prepared. When wings are formed in the egg, and no atmosphere provided to sustain them, — when eyes are fashioned in the womb, and no sun rises to meet them, — then may you believe that a nation worthy to survive is committed to an ordeal for which there are no resources, or insufficient ones.

Resources there are in this land, did we only draw upon them, which would close this war with the closing of this year.

INTO THIS CHASM AMERICA'S MANHOOD MUST LEAP.

It is not manhood that fights for its own freedom, holding itself ready to "crush with an iron hand" others who would seek their freedom.

It is not manhood that raises a question of rule over a question of Humanity.

It is not manhood that apologizes for every blow it is compelled to give to the greatest wrong against man.

It is not manhood that fears or distrusts the consequences of doing right.

When this becomes a war of our manhood, — i.e. a war for Humanity, — then the abyss will close; not before. Many treasures may be swallowed up ere that Curtius comes.

Americans! for the first time in many years you have an administration that really represents you. Your President is, by history and habit and sympathy, one of the people: he has not lived long enough in Washington to get on that political tripod which destroys the current of connection with the heart of the masses. However much individuals may be dissatisfied with the present management at Washington, there are many proofs that it represents the average *status* of the masses. As, then, we the people grow, it will grow; as our energy ripens, the Government will ripen. When Vallandigham is not sent from Ohio, his treason will not be tolerated at Washington. Be sure that the President will mirror your manhood when it arrives.

Bring forward the strength of your manhood, my countrymen, to whatever post of labor you are appointed! We need Ellsworths of the press, Winthrops of the fireside, Lyons of the pulpit. We need not only the brave men who shall defend the standards when they are lifted up, but earnest hearts who shall lift them up, — ay, upon the very towers of Humanity and Freedom. We need a banner on which every eye of the earth, looking, shall see written its freedom and joy. We need a school of seers, of prophets, who, as of old, shall cry aloud and spare not, showing the evils, the inhumanities, which must be conquered in ourselves, before we are worthy to fight for, and win, the victories of Right over Wrong, of Freedom over Slavery. Liberty's arm is not shortened that it cannot save; but our iniquities have come between us and that arm. Let every tongue that can speak be touched witn a live coal from the altar of God; let every pen that can write be dipped in the truest blood of an earnest heart; let every arm that can strike nerve itself to smite or be smitten for universal Freedom! Let none stand back, and say, "I will wait until this is a noble war,—a war for Humanity:" let all enter, and make it a noble war,—make it the struggle of Humanity. Our President is a Resolution which the people have passed. When a fresh and higher clause has been added by them, it will be repeated by every sword and cannon that goes southward from Washington. Whilst the water rises to but twenty feet with the people, let them not expect it to be thirty with their representatives. As we hold up their hands, or fail to hold them up, the day will be won or lost.

Forward, then, to the breach! No war of Manhood was ever yet lost.

The Rejected Stone, whose name is JUSTICE TO MAN, is, in the order of God, once more offered America. It is for the people to give it to the master-builder, to be laid as the Head of the Corner in the future fabric,—the Republic of Man.

That day, and that alone, which sees the Nation "broken" to the measure of this stone upon which it has now fallen, shall see its ONE FOE, upon which that stone shall then fall, GROUND TO POWDER.

XIX.

THE GREAT METHOD OF PEACE.

It were a sad thing if we should suffer the clangor of arms to drown that angel-choir that ever singeth of "Peace on earth, and good-will to men." We should indeed meet with utter indignation and execration that Devil's-peace, whose white flag now seeks to disguise the black one of the pirate and slaver, and to divide the forces that rally under that which alone now floats for Liberty and Justice. No war, however bloody or interminable, can be so horrible as that peace offered us by traitors in our midst, — a peace whose quiet would be that of a nation's grave, whose outside repose would be but the cover of corruption and loathsome vermin. Against *such* a peace God has for ever set his angel with the sword of flame. Between him and all wrong there can be no peace: the white flag of peace is only a flag of truce. The truce may last a month, a year, ten years; but between Justice and Injustice, Right and Wrong, Liberty and Slavery, there can only be a truce, — never a peace. The very field of conciliation invariably turns out the field of battle; for before the song of "Peace on earth!" comes that of "Glory to God in the highest!"

But, my friends, though not a thousandth part so bad

as a false peace, war is always wrong. It is sometimes, as now, necessary; but not absolutely, only relatively, necessary, — necessary, that is, only because we know not the things that make for our peace. There might be a peace at once,—a peace consistent with our national honor and unity; but the means of it are hid from our nation's eyes. Every rebel might be disarmed to-morrow. But the victories of Peace require so much more courage than those of war, that they are rarely won. When we do conquer a peace, however, it will assuredly be by the use of a certain sword, which, if drawn to-day, would win us a peace to-day, — a sword, too, which does not destroy, but makes alive.

Gregory of Tours walked near the palace of Soissons with Sylvius, the Bishop of Albi. "Do you see any thing on that roof?" said Sylvius. "I see the standard which Hilperic the king has set up," replied the monk. "And you see nothing else?" inquired the bishop. "No: do you see any thing?"—"I see the sword of Divine Vengeance hung over that wicked house."

So it proved; so it will ever prove. When human endurance is at an end, the sentence of Heaven is close at hand. Such sentence is indeed pronounced through human lips, and executed by human hands; but when, in an extremity, by the necessity that knows no law, or rather obeys the highest of laws, a people is driven to enact some mighty change in society, they consummate the decree of the Universe. By such revolution, God fulfils the oath he has sworn, that every wrong shall be overthrown, and the kingdoms of this world become the kingdom of his Christ for ever.

It does not require eyes so keen as those of the old French bishop to see the hair-strung sword of retribution hung over the palace of King Secession. While the North is now sending its young men to die on the battle-field, the sword, at the sight of which Rebellion would ground its arms, yet sleeps in the scabbard by our side. That sword is Emancipation. Fear or hate will inevitably draw it, in the end: how much better that Justice and Mercy should draw it now! The common sense of the nation has already rendered the verdict, that Slavery is the cause of this trouble; yet we have forborne to touch that institution. Not only is Slavery the historic cause of the Rebellion, but it is the one thing that alone makes it practicable at the South. Slavery is itself essentially, and in its most quiet condition, a rebellion. It is a rebellion against the laws of this Universe,—a guilty defiance of God and of man. So it stood in reason before it bore its bitter fruits in practice. Nettle-roots sting not; but 'tis their law to produce the nettles that do sting. Hence Slavery has not departed from its natural law in now seeking to lift its "bars" against "our banner in the sky." Its whole spirit and tendency is to engender that arrogance and self-aggrandizement which have culminated in this Rebellion. To enslave four millions is a suitable training for the enslavement of thirty. But, as we have said, it is not only the ultimate cause of

Secession: Slavery alone renders the present attitude of the South possible. It is only because a slave can be left at home to till the soil, that the white man is able to bear arms in the army. Should it be once announced, that every slave was, in the eye of the country, a free man, each Southerner would have to hurry home to be his own home-guard and his own home-provisioner. Such a measure would disband the Southern forces, and pin every rebel to his home. Their armies would soon "fold their tents, like the Arabs, and silently steal away." Every slave in the South, whether building breastworks or not, whether belonging to a loyalist or not, is, by the wealth and strength he produces in that section, really arrayed against the North. Some of us are hoping for an insurrection down there to demoralize their army. It will never come. Three fully armed watchmen can secure a hundred slaves from consultation or rising. Hercules will not come and take the wheel out of the rut for us. Nay, more: as long as we fail to use that weapon, it is one whose hilt may at any critical moment be grasped by the South, and wielded with terrible effect. The Republic of Colombia placed a sword in every slave's hand, and proclaimed freedom to each and all who should rally to its defence. The South may follow this example; and thus, by proving itself more the Negro's friend than the North, may turn our natural allies in their midst to our active and bitter foes. Dear as their slaves are to the South, the hope of conquering the "Yankees" is dearer; and they would gladly give up the half-million males which this would free to insure their triumph. Should they adopt this measure, we should be inevitably defeated in the war.

I feel profoundly impressed that the country should at once and most seriously look this matter in the face. In the rapid march of events, how soon may this sure weapon be carried beyond our reach! I therefore propose to look below the surface of this matter, and examine some of those popular errors concerning the policy of emancipation which have been industriously circulated and fostered by the defenders of Slavery, and which may yet paralyze our arm in the great moment of its opportunity. These errors pass daily from tongue to tongue on our streets, in such phrases as "the horrors of insurrection," "the scenes of St. Domingo;" and we are constantly asked, "What could we do with the Negroes?"

It is a little singular that Slavery has so long been able to keep up in the popular mind an idea that emancipation would bring all manner of evils and complications in its train, when the facts are so emphatically otherwise. The dictum is complacently announced in our midst, whilst nearly every civilized nation is at this moment enjoying the beneficent results of emancipation. Let us see:—

On the tenth day of October, 1811, the Congress of Chili decreed that every child born of slave parents after that date should be free.

On the 9th of April, 1812, the Government of Buenos Ayres declared the same free who should be born after the 1st of January, 1813.

On the 19th of July, 1821, the Congress of Colombia emancipated all the slaves who had borne arms for the defence of the Republic, and provided for the entire emancipation in eighteen years of all its slaves, — two hundred and eighty thousand in number.

On the 15th of September, 1821, Mexico granted immediate and unconditional emancipation to all its slaves.

On the 4th of July, 1827, the State of New York emancipated at once its ten thousand slaves.

On the 1st of August, 1834, Great Britain emancipated, at a cost of a hundred million dollars, all the slaves in her West-Indian possessions, — eight hundred thousand in number.

Here, now, are instances of every variety of emancipation, — immediate, gradual, conditional, unconditional; and it has not only yet to be shown where and when any scene of violence or danger followed these decrees, in even a single instance, but it can be shown that each of these countries rose after them in the national scale as to security and general prosperity. This has been particularly the case in the West Indies, about which so many lies have been so industriously circulated. There, on one glorious night, eight hundred thousand slaves knelt in their chapels, watching for Liberty's midnight-morning; and, when the midnight hour rang out, they arose *freemen*. The morning's dawn found each one at his usual post of labor, and ready to continue to earn the legitimate produce of the island. There were scenes of joy such as might have drawn the gaze of hovering angels; there were such touching scenes as must attend the casting-aside of grave-clothes, — the emergence from the sepulchre of a people who have heard a Messiah saying, "Come forth! Unbind him, hand and foot!" But there was not one scene of that rebellion and retribution which had been anticipated, perhaps because merited.

But we hear much of the "fearful scenes of St. Domingo." I have reserved mention of this island, because it contains for us a higher lesson than the practicability of emancipation (which it also teaches); even the formidable results which may follow an attempt to thwart the policy of emancipation when any exigency commands it. There is, indeed, a possibility that "the scenes of St. Domingo" may be repeated upon this continent; and it is not hard to foretell on whom the responsibility of their occurrence shall rest in such an event.

On the 28th of March, 1790, the National Assembly of France decreed that "all free persons" of St. Domingo should have the right of suffrage. This was passed at the solicitation of the free colored residents of the island, and was meant to confer the privilege of voting upon them. The planters became excessively indignant at this grant of political privileges to the free Negroes, and denied them the right to avail themselves of it. Ogé, a mulatto, claimed the exercise of the right at the head of an army. A war-cry was the response. At length, the planters, after the death of six thousand men, acquiesced; the French Assembly meanwhile inserting the word "colored" in their decree of suffrage, so as to make its grant to the free Negroes unmistakable. Thus far, there was no attempt by any party to free the slaves: indeed, the free Negroes had helped at various times to suppress the insurrection of slaves against those very planters with whom they were themselves contending. In September, 1791, the French Government revoked the decree of suffrage to the free Negroes. It was doubtless as an expedient: for, on the 4th of April of the next year, the decree of rights was again issued, and three commissioners with six thousand troops sent by France to St. Domingo to enforce it. Thereupon the planters inaugurated a conspiracy to place their island in the hands of England. The French commissioners, hearing of the approach of English troops, and finding that they must resist an assault from that power with about twenty-one thousand troops, on three-fourths of which (they being the militia of the country) they could not rely, emancipated the slaves, — five hundred thousand in number: a measure which France and England may yet, in the same way, compel the United States to adopt. The British evacuation of St. Domingo took place in 1798. Then Toussaint l'Ouverture became the black Washington of his country, securing the unity and independence of St. Domingo in 1801.

Let it be remembered, that, up to this time, there were no "fearful scenes" in St. Domingo, except such as were occasioned by an insane rebellion of the white planters against the just decrees of their government; and each fresh horror came of their mad conspiracy to transfer the island to foreign powers. The slaves, after their manumission by the French Commissioners, went on for the most part working patiently as before, seeking no political privileges, until this quiet was changed by the conspiracies of the planters to betray them, now to this nation, now to that, — to any that would re-enslave them. When their liberties were assaulted by Napoleon eight years after they were legally gained, these men showed themselves worthy of those liberties by defending them, as brave men have done in every age and land; but, with the exception of the massacre ordered by Dessalines, — which should be laid at his own door, most of the Negroes recoiling from it, — the whole history of the Haitian Republic down to this day is a continuous record and attestation of French and English and Spanish treacheries and cruelties, — perfidies and cruelties persistent and almost incredible, — and of heroism, patience, and only too much generosity, on the part of the Negroes.

Indeed, there never was a siege or campaign of one of these white nations which was not followed by outrages, for the cruelty of which the records of insurrection furnish no parallel. In even the insurrection of Nat Turner, in Virginia, the violation of woman formed no part. In the plan of Denmark Vesey, in South Carolina, there was a stern prohibition against any wanton outrage; and not a blow was aimed but would have been essential to liberation. No woman or child was ever slain, except it was certain they would be able to alarm neighborhoods, and defeat the plan of insurrection; and the blow, wherever it fell, was swift, the death instant, where in other lands vindictive tortures have been resorted to. The motto of the Negro, in the few instances where he has struck for his freedom, has always been "*Liberty,*" never "*Vengeance.*" In this regard, the mildest race in the world has been most infamously slandered, or absurdly misunderstood.

As far as any minds are haunted by the question, "What shall we do with the Negroes, should we free them?" we have to say, that we should do with them just what was done in the seven cases of modern times already named, in each of which the same question, "What shall we do with them?" cleared away like a phantom before the dawn of emancipation. The measure was followed in each case by no evil, and by every happy result. With the South, indeed, as with others, the palaces of the few might shrink; but the huts of the many would expand to homes of comfort. Immense plantations would become smaller; but the little patch of ground that scarcely sustains the poor white of the South would be enlarged. And with this whole false state of society would pass away the effeminacy, the licentiousness, the arrogance, and general barbarism, which are the legitimate brood of Slavery, and which have shown their power to make the fairest and broadest country of the earth a cage of unclean birds.

There is one lesson that the Negro temperament easily learns, and one which a long training has confirmed; that is, obedience. He *may* presently become a blind insurrectionist, and his wrath sweep like a conflagration through the land: we shall then see that it was a false mercy to the South, and a great injustice to the whole country, that he was not (as he may be now) transformed into a controllable power and subject of the nation.

As far as their able-bodied workmen are concerned, there is plenty for them to do. Our broad lands North and South need their labor as much as ever. As far as the many aged and the children and invalids — who at present, without risk, could not remain in the South — are concerned, we should be more fortunate than any emancipating nation ever was before. Haiti sits at this moment waiting to help this great work; willing to send her every ship to our shores, and bear to hers every Negro who will go. The Queen of the Antilles sits on her throne of plenty, — her land gilded with richest fruits, calling only for hands to gather and turn them into wealth, — offering every colored man who will come the bounty of a free voyage thither, and a land-grant on his arrival. With one word of recognition, this Government can secure at once the peace and safety of both Haiti and America.*

Is it not melancholy that nations so generally wait to be driven by hard physical necessity to do great and just deeds? The just measure, which, if done from a high motive and in calmness, produces pure and beneficent results to all, if done afterward, under the compulsion of fear or as a measure of vengeance, brings those results fearfully alloyed with difficulties and dangers. The work that God gives us to do, we do a great deal better than it will be done if we send it back for him to do. What the French Assembly might have written peacefully on parchment, but refused, God soon after wrote with a pen of iron, and in blood-red ink, on every

* It is almost unpardonable, indeed, that our Government has not already spoken that word; and the failure may be attributed chiefly to the fact, that we have nobody whose business it is to attend to such matters. It may be said, just here, that it is high time that another department in our Government should be recognized and formally created; one whose duty should be a suitable attention to the Slavery question, and to the momentous and complex affairs growing out of it day by day. We need a new Cabinet officer for this. It is of infinitely more importance than the Bureau for the Indians. The Government has already drifted hopelessly, and without any certain policy, amidst the fragments and snags of this half-wrecked institution, — one policy in Missouri, another in Virginia. Let the peril be provided for at once. It may be, before long, seen that the issue of our country's life or death rests with the Slavery question. Already it is generally felt, that, whilst there is the utmost need that we should have a policy on the matter to which we can adhere, there is a painful confusion of thought among the people, and of action among their rulers, as to what is, or should be, the attitude of our Government toward that institution. Let the Government re-assure the public, by making it certain that we shall not be wrecked on this rock for want of a special pilot to watch and warn.

street in Paris. When we leave it to Providence to do our work, Providence always brings with it a mixture of hell-fire, to teach the foolish world how much better it is to do its own work. The abolition of Slavery, which is almost inevitable during this war, would, if accomplished at this moment, unselfishly and grandly, simply because the war-power has brought the nation to the one glorious moment when it *can legally abolish it*, be a peace measure: ere long it will be a fierce and fearful war measure, almost as painful to the party forced to use it as to those at whom it will be aimed.

Ah! if this nation but knew, in this its day, the things that belong to its peace! Now they are hid from its eyes. Hid; but not because they are not just before us; not because it is too late to avail ourselves of them: they are hid because our eyes are weak and averted, not having the courage to look squarely before us. Glorious as our national uprising has been, it has not yet reached that pure and peaceful elevation, that, with a wave of the divine wand of rectitude, could sway without a blow the muttering Caliban of Rebellion.

An old man lately looked upon the pale, dead face of his slain son, and said, "Slavery, then, has thus entered my own door." Into how many doors has it come! Already within six months, some ten thousand young men of America have been sacrificed on the unholy altar of human bondage. Already stalwart arms are idle, Trade languishes at her marts, and the cry of the poor at the North begins to answer that of the oppressed at the South: together their voices cry to God and man, asking, "Men and brethren, what great good has this institution ever done, what good is it now doing or expected to do, that would make it desirable to sacrifice a single human life to it, much less thousands of lives? What is there in Slavery that would make it well to sacrifice to it the bread of one weeping child, much less the living of thousands? Why, oh! why, this cruel tenacity to an unmitigated evil, and one which alone makes this war possible? Does it make the slaveholder a good man, or a wise and peaceful and happy man? Does it make freemen noble, brave, devoted to the right? Does it add to the nation's wealth, culture, progress, or happiness? Is it not an unmitigated and blighting curse, now heavy upon every man, woman, and child in this land? Look, then, America, into the pallid faces of thy slain young men; follow from home to home where the destroying angel has passed; listen to the growing cry for work, already changing to the fiercer cry for bread; see paralyzed trade and closed schools; and tell us what there is in human oppression so sacred that its blood-splashed chariot-wheels must not be stayed."

We all see plainly that our Government is led by the people, and that the people must first pass the great acts which must guide their rulers. This has always been the case where any great and solemn crisis, involving high moral principles, has arrived to a nation. Diplomatists and politicians never strike a great blow for the right, except from the constraining force of public opinion: the wrong they do is spontaneous. If they must do right, they take care to explain that it is from military or political necessity; but they seem never to fear that a measure will not be supported because of its unrighteousness. The heart of England was absolutely all aflame and seething against Slavery in the West Indies, whilst the Government was cold and impassive. One day, the petitions for emancipation were so numerous and bulky, that it took six men to carry them into Parliament. Then Parliament stirred a little. One day afterward, it was reported that eight hundred thousand women of England — one for every slave in the West Indies — were knocking at the door of Parliament, and demanding the emancipation of the slaves. Then the Government sent them word: "Go to your homes; the slave is free."

There is no reason why Americans should not be as earnest and persistent as their English relatives. There is no reason why we should not have our six men to carry in our petitions for emancipation into the next Congress, and our eight hundred thousand or four million women besieging the Government for that peace which can alone repose on justice.

Many a young man is asking in these times, "How can I best befriend my country?" Young man! you can befriend it by letting your manhood utter itself in word and deed; by bearing with your whole weight, howsoever you can make it felt, for the liberation of the slave, which now means the liberation and peace of your country. Many a noble woman yearns to serve in some post of duty, and complains in her secret soul of the hard fate that seems to shut her out from places of active usefulness. Women! remember those who were "last at the cross, and earliest at the sepulchre;" remember those eight hundred thousand women who wrung from England that bright First of August, — the Coronal Day of Nations; and swear a sacred oath to-day, that your prayer shall be heard in the Capitol of this nation, imploring liberty and justice for the slave, — the things that belong to our country's peace.

THE END.

www.ingramcontent.com/pod-product-compliance
Lightning Source LLC
LaVergne TN
LVHW021420110826
845150LV00007B/2010

9781425509248